The CRAFT of Assessment

MICHAEL CHILES

First published 2020

by John Catt Educational Ltd,
15 Riduna Park, Station Road,
Melton, Woodbridge IP12 1QT

Tel: +44 (0) 1394 389850
Fax: +44 (0) 1394 386893
Email: enquiries@johncatt.com
Website: www.johncatt.com

ISBN: 978 1 912906 81 9

Set and designed by John Catt Educational Limited

PRAISE FOR 'THE CRAFT OF ASSESSMENT'

'The CRAFT of Assessment is a superbly executed book. Establishing an effective process of assessment and feedback is one of the most difficult aspects of teaching and this book contains a wealth of insights and ideas for getting it right. I love how the research background quickly leads into concrete practical strategies that are interwoven with teachers' real experiences through the teacher spotlights. Real examples of student work and teachers' formative assessment and feedback strategies bring the ideas alive in a way that few books manage to do. This will be a great addition to any school's CPD library and should be widely read and shared.'
– **Tom Sherrington (@teacherhead), Founder of Teacherhead Consulting and author of *Rosenshine's Principles of Action* and *The Learning Rainforest***

'Drawing on a wide range of expertise, evidence and research as well as the authors' own experiences, all of the content covered in this book will be of use and value to those who work in schools, regardless of age range or subject, as it focuses on key aspects that are vital to teaching and learning. In addition to the discussion of widely-discussed topics, such as different forms of feedback and retrieval practice strategies, there is also sound advice on areas not as widely discussed, such as effective PowerPoint design and how to communicate learning intentions.

Well referenced and with a fascinating range of case studies in the form of teacher spotlights featuring classroom educators further adds to the authentic voice of this book, learning from those sharing their experiences from the classroom. Teachers and leaders alike will love this book and find it helpful for improving their own practice and/or supporting others too.'
– **Kate Jones (@87history), author of Retrieval Practice and Love to Teach, Head of History at The British School Al Khubairat, Abu Dhabi**

'The CRAFT of Assessment is a meticulously researched publication; rammed full of practical examples and advice that will undoubtedly become a 'go to' book for teachers of any experience in any context. In each chapter, education theory comes alive through teacher spotlights in which expert practitioners share their wisdom and insights into day to day teaching. These invaluable case studies are an essential starting point for those teachers who wish to focus on a specific aspect of their daily practice in order to become even better.

Each chapter is informative, well laid out and referenced, allowing for possible further exploration of the detailed pedagogical approaches. However, the book is so comprehensive that additional sources may not be required. The final chapter focuses on establishing a culture of learning and if instructional coaching is your thing then this book will provide you and your colleagues with multiple solutions and action steps. The only problem is what to focus on first! Whatever you decide this book will have it covered.'

– Chris Moyse, Head of Staff Development for Bridgwater and Taunton College Trust and Managing Director, TLC Education Services Ltd

'Seamlessly combining a wealth of practical ideas with research-informed explanations, this book is a must read. Mike's years of experience as a classroom teacher shine through in this book that will simultaneously challenge your thinking, force you to try out new ideas and fall in love with the CRAFT of teaching.'

– Kate Stockings (@Kate_Stockings), Head of Geography at Hampstead School, speaker and author of geography resources

'If you are looking for a book that places assessment at the heart of great pedagogy then look no further. Michael Chiles has skilfully curated the latest research into classroom assessment and combined it with a fabulous range of on-the-ground contributions from serving teachers to create a book brimming with practical ideas that are rooted in proven practice. With its helpful focus on assessment as a tool designed primarily to promote growth not measure progress, it's basically AFL on steroids! Highly recommend.'

– Andy Buck, speaker, coach and author of
***Leadership Matters* and *Honk*!**

CONTENTS

ACKNOWLEDGEMENTS

Firstly, a big thank you to my wife Sarah Thornton for being the critical ear as the book unfolded and for her unconditional love and support, always.

Secondly, a heartfelt thank you to my grandad Ralph whose love and wisdom throughout my childhood inspired me to be the teacher and person I am today. This book is dedicated to you.

I would like to thank Simon Turney, my first headteacher as I started my teaching career who supported me and gave me my first leadership opportunity.

Lastly, this book is brought to life by the spotlights from Rosemin Mitha, Kirsty Barker, Ben Ranson, Sarah Larsen, Zoe Enser, Dr Flavia Belham, Dawn Cox, Aidan Severs, Jack Tavassoly-Marsh, Sam Strickland. A big thank you for sharing your experiences, along with Mark Enser for his foreword.

FOREWORD BY MARK ENSER

When I started teaching at the beginning of the millennium, assessment was the issue on everyone's lips. It was a time when the work of Dylan Wiliam and Paul Black on formative assessment, 'assessment for learning', was taking hold and the majority of our CPD in those years was spent getting to grips with this exciting new idea. You might have hoped that in the proceeding two decades, following all this work, assessment would have been something that we, as a profession, had cracked. This does not seem to be the case.

The removal of national curriculum levels in 2014 helped to reveal a gap in our collective 'assessment literacy'. Schools and teachers up and down the country struggled to work out how to replace the use of these levels when assessing and tracking pupils and most ended up simply recreating them in another form and/or creating 'flight paths' to track whether pupils were on route to hit some sort of ill-defined GCSE target many years hence.

At the heart of our problems with assessment sits an uneasy truth; that we have never seized back the purpose of assessment from outside forces. Too often assessment is done to collect data that can go on a spreadsheet. Data demanded for some sort of use outside the classroom, whether to pacify parents, school leaders or – in the past – inspectors. Assessment has, despite all the work on assessment for learning, largely sat outside of teaching and learning as something that teachers have had to *do* but then have not really had to *make use of*. Assessment wasn't for us.

What Michael Chiles has done with CRAFT is integrate assessment into the discourse around pedagogy more generally. He brings assessment back into the classroom as a tool used by teachers – a thread in the tapestry of classroom practice woven by the teacher and their class. Assessment becomes a central part of the teacher's role, not in a desire simply to measure, but as a means of making something grow. In this model, assessment becomes a way of gaining insight into what Graham Nuthall termed the 'hidden lives of learners'. Assessment allows us to catch a glimpse of what is otherwise the invisible process of learning.

Once we, as teachers, have taken back control of assessment and used it with the sole purpose of informing us about what has been learnt, we are then free to make use of this information. We can provide pupils with feedback designed not to improve a particular piece of work but to improve subsequent work. We can use the information to inform our teaching of a topic in the future and to let us know whether pupils are ready to move on or whether we need to revisit something that we now know pupils never really learnt. This book seeks to empower teachers to take this kind of control over assessment in its widest sense and, therefore, over the rest of our practice.

This is a generous book in many regards. It builds on and gives thanks to those whose principles on teaching, learning and assessment shape classroom practice today. It is also generous in terms of its contributions from a wide range of teachers of various subjects and of various phases of education. Finally, it is a generous book in terms of the practical advice and concrete examples that are provided. Whereas other books on education fall back on vague – if well meaning – platitudes, Michael always gives the specific detail that working teachers need.

This is very much a teacher's book. It provides the authentic voice of a member of a profession that is still grappling with the complex issue of assessment. This is a voice grounded in research and theory but always elevated by the reality of classroom practice. It is time to welcome meaningful assessment back to the classroom.

Mark Enser is Head of Geography and Research Lead at Heathfield Community College. He is also an author, speaker and columnist.

INTRODUCTION

Teaching: 'The act, process, or art of imparting knowledge and skill.'[1]

Learning: 'An alternation in long-term memory.'[2]

Teaching is one of the most rewarding careers; every day provides its own unique challenges as we take the younger generation on a learning journey, imparting the knowledge they require to gain an understanding of the rich tapestry of our subjects that enable them to become lifelong learners.

The education climate is somewhat different compared to when I first started as an NQT, 13 years ago. While the expectations of classroom teachers and leaders has been on a continual change during this time, I firmly believe we are entering a decade where there is a real desire from teachers to become evidenced-informed to create greater opportunities that will help improve the life chances of the pupils in front of them on daily basis.

In summary, I believe the key ingredients when planning a lesson fall under the following headings:

- Teaching to the top
- Scaffolding up
- Asking lots of questions
- Modelling excellence

1. Collins Dictionary. (2020) 'Teaching', Collins Dictionary [Online]. Retrieved from: www.bit.ly/3aWl3fR
2. Kirschner, P. A., Sweller, J. and Clark, R. E. (2006) 'Why Minimal Guidance During Instruction Does Not Work: An Analysis of the Failure of Constructivist, Discovery, Problem-Based, Experiential, and Inquiry-Based Teaching', *Educational Psychologist* 41 (2) pp. 75-86.

- Checking for understanding
- Activating lots of retrieval, which is spaced
- Providing timely feedback that enables pupils to feedforward to close the gap

In each of the chapters, I will outline the research-based evidence for each aspect of CRAFT, strategies that teachers can use in and out of the classroom, as well as spotlights from teachers across a broad range of phases and subjects to share how they have implemented an element of CRAFT in their own classrooms.

In Chapter 1, the C of CRAFT, I will consider the big question, how can knowledge be effectively condensed? Delving into the role that teachers can have in supporting pupils to condense learning to create powerful notes and take ownership of their learning. Thus, providing them with the platform to transform new learning into memorable materials that can be used to rehearse and deliberately practice. In the two spotlights for this chapter, Rosemin Guerrero Mitha, a RE and psychology teacher and Kirsty Barker, a dance teacher, share how they have supported pupils in condensing learning.

In Chapter 2, the R of CRAFT, I will outline the research into generating reflective learners and how teachers at both primary and secondary phases can create opportunities for pupils in and out of the classroom to strengthen memory connections through the combined use of the learning strategies of retrieval and spaced practice. Therefore, allowing pupils to deliberately practice retrieval to improve long-term memory and knowledge recall throughout their learning journey. For the spotlights in this chapter, Ben Ranson, a geography teacher and Dr Flavia Belham, Chief Scientist at Seneca Learning, share their experiences on generating reflective learners.

In Chapter 3, the A of CRAFT, I will consider the debate on the historical use of assessment to check for understanding and argue that the use of levels and grades have inevitably distorted the real value behind the role of assessment for learning to support teachers and pupils in developing a deeper understanding of what they know, what they need to know and how they can get there. In this chapter, this is exemplified through the shared experiences of Dawn Cox, an RE teacher and Aidan Severs, a senior leader in the primary phase through their spotlights.

In Chapter 4, the F and T of CRAFT, I will explore the research-based evidence on the combination of the use of feedforward and feedback, as well as the strategies to provide pupils with positive and specific targets to close the knowledge gaps. Spotlights from Sarah Larsen and Jack Tavassoly-Marsh – both geography teachers – and Zoe Enser – an English teacher and now teaching and learning leader – exemplify this.

In Chapter 5, I will look at the research on the use of instructional coaching to support teachers in implementing, reviewing and supporting colleagues in implementing the use of effective strategies to develop their CRAFT of teaching. In the final spotlight, Sam Strickland a current headteacher of a secondary school shares his thoughts on creating a culture of learning.

My main desire to write this book was foremost to share my experiences as a practising classroom practitioner, provide busy teachers and leaders with an outline of some key findings from research, as well as to suggest some practical strategies that could be implemented to support other teachers in their own CRAFT of teaching. I hope this book provides a platform to support your development as a teacher and leader.

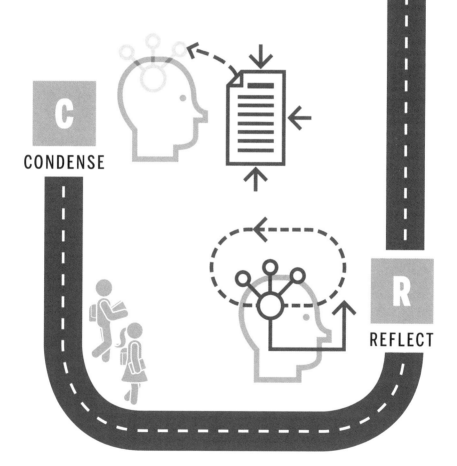

CRAFT

C CONDENSE

R REFLECT

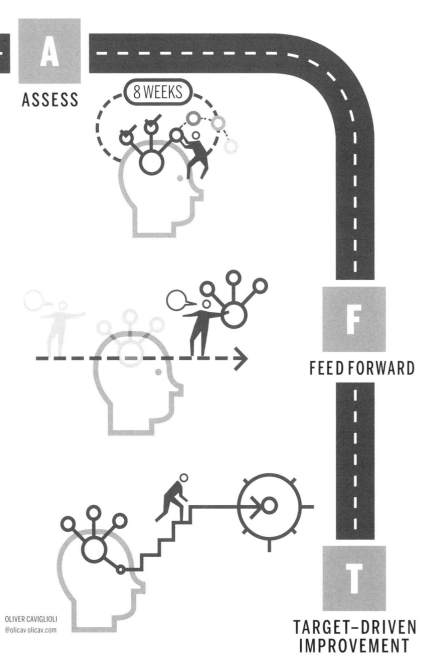

ASSESS

8 WEEKS

FEED FORWARD

TARGET-DRIVEN
IMPROVEMENT

1

THE 'C': HOW CAN KNOWLEDGE BE EFFECTIVELY CONDENSED?

OLIVER CAVIGLIOLI
@olicav olicav.com

Abigail, a Year 10 pupil, is nearing the end of the first year of her GCSEs. She is a conscientious pupil who wants to achieve the highest grades across all her subjects by the end of Year 11. She regularly reads over her class notes from her exercise book and highlights the keywords, as well as using the recommended revision guides and workbooks suggested by her subject teachers. She spends time every week reading the textbooks and making extra notes. However, when it comes to using these notes, she is overwhelmed by the amount that she needs to revise.

How many times have pupils said to you that they learn better from reading and re-reading their classroom notes and highlighting them, or reading revision guides and textbooks? When pupils conduct this type of revision, they often perceive that they are effectively revising by re-reading and highlighting previous notes or paragraphs from publications. This is because the act of reading over the same information numerous times creates a feel-good factor when they remember isolated chunks of knowledge based on what they had previously read. This inevitably leads to a subconscious belief that learning has taken place. There are numerous studies demonstrating that when pupils read and re-read textbooks it takes time and has little to no impact on improving long-term retention of the information.[1] Alongside this belief there are a wealth of revision resources through revision guides, workbooks, flashcards, quizzes that allow pupils to reflect on previously studied knowledge. Whilst these revision guides and workbooks provide opportunities for reflection and practice, during the course of their GCSEs, we want pupils to be able to generate powerful condensed notes of their own that they can draw upon and use to revisit, review and reflect on knowledge learnt. The art of reflection is something I explore further in Chapter 2. For now, let's consider how knowledge can be presented, encoded and condensed to support the learning process.

The memory model is now well documented and shared in the education sphere, so I won't spend too long revisiting the theory. However, as with any research, 'knowing' the theory is just one aspect, it is also about finding the most effective strategies for your pupils to implement the theory to support learning. The driving force of our intellectual performance is knowledge, which is stored in schematic form in our long-term memory. We know from the work around the research into the memory model that our working memory is the place where we process the information we receive as we go about our daily lives and the capacity of it is small. Scientists believe that our working memory can only process 3-4 items of information at once and this can only be held for around 20-30 seconds, without rehearsal. Too much information can cause cognitive overload. In comparison, we know from research that our long-term memory is far vaster and can store an infinite amount of information. For learning to take place we want information to be transferred to our long-term memory for recall in the future. When presenting new concepts and processes in a sequence of learning we should be considered how we present this information to support pupils in processing it and enabling them to condense learning into powerful notes.

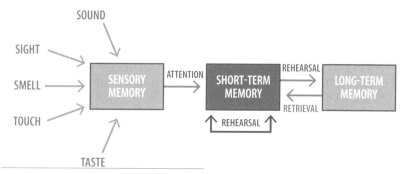

1. Weinstein, Y., Sumeracki, M. and Caviglioli, O. (2018) *Understanding How We Learn: A Visual Guide*. Abingdon, Oxon: Routledge, p.33.

Cognitive load can be characterised by three different types: intrinsic load, extraneous load and germane load.

- Intrinsic load relates to the complexity of the information that is being learnt, which is influenced by pupil's prior knowledge.
- Extraneous load is imposed by the way in which the material is presented, which doesn't help pupils to learn and we should aim to keep this as low as possible.
- German load originates from the designing of instruction that has a direct influence on schema construction. This is important because it directly supports learning.

Condensing the PowerPoint

When considering how we present knowledge to pupils in lessons, we should be mindful of not overloading working memory, which may result in pupils finding it difficult to process and encode the information presented. During my early teaching career, the PowerPoint presentation was a security blanket for delivering lessons. It got to a point that if I didn't have a PowerPoint presentation ready, then I hadn't planned my lesson and, therefore, I wouldn't be able to deliver the intended outcome. In more recent years, the reliance on PowerPoint presentations with lots of transition and information crowded onto one slide can become an unnecessary distraction that can remove a cog from the mechanics of your intended expert explanation. To create the most effective opportunities to deliver precision in our explanations so that pupils can process, encode and condense, we should be mindful of how we use PowerPoint presentations. Andy Tharby shared some advice on how teachers could their use:

- Less is more – reduce the amount of text and diagrams to as little as is necessary. It may seem counterintuitive, but when students are working with new and complex material, the more jam-packed your slides, the less likely they are to learn.
- Ensure that labels are integrated into diagrams – so that students can look at text and images simultaneously.
- Remove distracting or superfluous images – only use those that directly support learning.
- Use arrows to show connections between text and diagrams.
- Use colour coding to show the relationship between connected ideas, but avoid the use of *too many* colours.
- Ensure that the information is presented physically close to related information.

- Use images to support complex and conceptual ideas. The dual coding theory suggests that presenting language and images together assists learning.
- If you intend to explain an image, it is best not to include written text at the same time.
- Avoid reading out text that is already written on the slide.
- Never expect student to read something while you are talking at the same time.
- Reveal processes stage-by-stage on the same slide, rather than consecutive slides. This way, students have a prompt to remind them of earlier stages and can catch up if they lose concentration for the moment.
- Remember that spoken words and slides are fleeting and transient and that your students' innate cognitive architecture means that they will be unable to hold onto them all at once. Slideshow handouts and directed note taking can reduce this problem.[2]

When I think back to my geography lessons, I don't picture an expertly executed presentation, I picture quite the opposite, that of my old geography teacher Mr Byrne sharing his expert knowledge of the world with passion and precision. When delivering new information to our pupils we should consider what I believe are the four cogs to expert explanation that will contribute towards pupils learning.

COG 1 – PASSION

It occurred to me a few years ago, while watching Hans Rosling deliver his presentations on our ever-evolving world, there was something about his delivery, his passion for the subject, that left me waiting on his every word. He would suddenly change the pitch and speed of his voice, emphasising certain words, as he would build the anticipation of the explanation before revealing the answer. This delivery kept me captivated and wanting to know more, which I believe is important when instilling rich knowledge to students. In the classroom, this comes through our ability as teachers to tell stories and use concrete examples to allow students to relate to difficult concepts and processes.

---

2. Tharby, A. (2018) 'Using cognitive load theory to improve slide show presentations', *Durrington Research School* [Online] 19 April. Retrieved from: www.bit.ly/39pKqWX

COG 2 – PRECISION

The dreaded MOT test, an annual uncertainty as to whether we have successfully ensured our vehicle is roadworthy. We want to know the answer to the ultimate question, has it passed? If not, we expect that the mechanic will be able to diagnose the problem and sort it, using their expertise. When we are delivering an expert explanation to our students, we need to know the mechanics of our subject; we need to be the experts. Therefore, the delivery of knowledge to the students in front of us should be done with precision, reducing the extraneous load by removing unnecessary information and 'sticking to the point'.

COG 3 – REHEARSE

In the early stages of my career lesson planning involved lengthy two to three pages of a step-by-step script of what would happen in the lesson. I remember the more experienced teachers looking in bemusement, referring to the more orthodox phrase of 'fag packet planning'. It was of no surprise after several years that I realised a two to three-page lesson plan was not a productive use of my time and the outcomes I was expecting from students ended up being very much the opposite. I'm not saying that teachers shouldn't be planning lessons, instead I believe it is important that we plan and craft out the delivery of our explanation. After all, if we can deliver an explanation with passion and precision, we have a greater chance of captivating our students. I remember a few years ago sitting through a workshop with Chris Moyse (@ChrisMoyse) and he said something that has remained with me ever since, 'do the same thing, but better'. I often use a blank piece of paper when planning my explanation and use CPD time with the department to practise the delivery of our explanations, especially with concepts that students struggle to understand. The more we rehearse our explanations the more captivating they will be.

COG 4 – DELIVERY

This, for me, is the most fundamental cog in expert explanation, the delivery, which is why rehearsing is crucial. The research on our working memory is important to consider when delivering an explanation because even with a passionate and precision pitch, we can quickly cause cognitive overload. This is where Barak Rosenshine's 'Principle of Instructions' is key to smooth delivery. Rosenshine's study outlines the importance of delivering explanations step by step, each one building on the next, 'the most successful teachers did not overwhelm their students by presenting too much new material at one time, and they taught in such a way that each point was mastered before the next point was introduced.' Therefore, our explanations should be seen as chapters of knowledge that should be presented over time to ensure that students are guided through difficult concepts and processes.

Cornell notes

Over the course of their studies pupils make notes in their exercise books and complete the set activities. How many times have pupils gone back to refer to their classroom notes to proclaim, 'I don't understand what we were actually doing that lesson!' Or, my class notes are not helpful for me to revise from. Is there a revision guide I can use to prepare for my exam? One key element of CRAFT is supporting pupils in creating condensed knowledge that focuses on what they need to know and provides a powerful reflective tool when it comes to review and reflecting on them over time. Something we explore in more depth in Chapter 2 on the R of CRAFT.

One strategy to support effectively and condensed note taking is the Cornell notes system, which involves the use of three sections to separate information from the lesson. One large section to include the main concept and processes, a column on the left for keywords and questions, and at the bottom of the page a section to summarise the key learning points in a short paragraph.

Notes	Keywords/comments	Summary

When it comes to organising and taking notes a key element of CRAFT is for teachers to provide pupils with the opportunity to organise notes, so that it allows them to reflect on learning effectively. The use of Cornell notes allows pupils to focus on the key chunks of knowledge that they should revisit and reflect on to improve their longer-term retention. The left-hand column is particularly useful for pupils to clarify meanings of key concepts and processes that they have been taught in the lesson, along with considering questions that they may have relating to any relationships or links to the main knowledge points from the lesson. This process of reflecting and reviewing the knowledge points can help strengthen memory. It also provides a clear structure for their notes so that when they come back to review the knowledge from the lesson it is clearly organised and allows for greater clarity of what they need to reflect on. I regularly get my pupils to summarise the learning from the lesson at the end of the lesson or when they take their books home to use for homework. The act of reviewing their notes provides the conditions for those pupils to perform typically higher in relation to outcomes than those that don't.

The use of Cornell notes in the classroom requires deliberate practice by teachers and pupils to embed a cohesive approach that supports learning. Like with any strategy, it is the modelling from the teacher and opportunities for deliberate practice that will support the implementation of the skill of note taking. Whilst it is more common for pupils in higher education settings to be taking notes during a lecture, this doesn't mean that the use of this note taking structure cannot be utilised in classrooms in A Level and GCSE settings. The key to improving pupils note taking skills is to teach them how to make effectively condensed notes.

Revision cards

Revision cards are useful tool for pupils to use when reflecting on their learning. How to use the revision cards effectively to reflect on learning is something I explore later in Chapter 2. For now, let's consider how we can guide pupils to create revision cards to condense learning and support them in using the cards to support and strengthen long-term memory. When it comes to creating the revision cards there are a few points to consider, to guide pupils when they are creating these cards:

1. On the front of the card pupils should write a key term or question. For example, in science this might be the word 'photosynthesis' or, in English, how does Scrooge's character change in the novel?
2. On the back of the card, pupils would write the answer to the definition or question.
3. Each revision card should focus on one key aspect of knowledge, rather than multiple concepts or processes.

Here's an example illustrating a geography revision card for the erosional process of attrition:

ATTRITION	The action of rock fragments colliding into each other causing them to become smaller and rounder over time.

Revision clocks

The revision clock, originally created by Becky Green (@teachgeogblog), is an excellent strategy to encourage pupils to condense the key concepts and processes for a topic into a one-page A3 summary. A guide on how pupils can approach the use of a revision clock is illustrated below:

MASTERING THE REVISION CLOCK

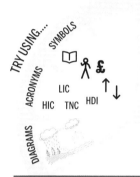

E.g.

What is the purpose? It is a way to condense class notes down into a visual summary of each topic, doing this makes for easy reference to refresh your memory before an exam.

Tropical rainforests have distinct characteristics that support a wide variety of different species. This means that they have a high biodiversity.
Becomes....
TRF's - ↑ biodiversity.

What does a good one look like?
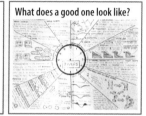

TOP TIPS

Be concise: Eliminate the unnecessary, in depth revision comes from revision guides and class books.
Save space: Replace words with symbols, shorten words or use acronyms to cram in the info.
Stand out: Using diagrams and pictures in place of lengthy explanations makes the information stand out.
Save keywords: When condensing the content, remember that keywords are KEY.

As with any form of condensing, pupils need to have accurate notes and models to demonstrate how to present knowledge in this format. The revision clocks provide both an opportunity for pupils to condense chunks of knowledge into the five-minute sections of the sheet, as well as using it to reflect on previous knowledge, the 'R' of CRAFT.

Graphic organisers

Graphic organisers support pupils in organising knowledge to build a visual map or diagram that allows them to see the relationships between concepts and processes. There are a variety of different types of graphic organisers that pupils can use depending on the type of knowledge they are organising and condensing. The organisation of knowledge is important because it can aid pupils in their future recall to aid long-term memory.

The work on dual coding with teachers by Oliver Caviglioli has been fantastic in bringing to the forefront how teachers organise and present knowledge to pupils, as well as supporting pupils in organising their own knowledge. Oliver outlines four ways graphic organisers can be used: chunk, compare, sequence, and cause and effect.

The following table demonstrate a couple of examples from across the different subjects on how pupils could use the different type of graphic organisers outlined by Oliver to condense learning.

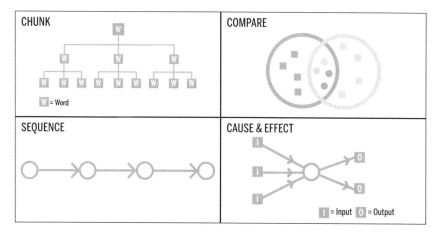

When using graphic organisers spend time explaining to pupils the type of organiser that they should use and the reasons why this is the most appropriate one. Provide models of what the graphic organiser should look like when complete and provide the time for deliberate practice to embed this as a successful strategy for condensing knowledge.

Infographics

Another way pupil's can condense learning into powerful notes is through infographics. Infographics are constructed by using graphic information, visual graphic information, core knowledge or data, and when constructed together can create a succinct representation of an aspect of a topic that is being studied. In 2013, Vanichvasin indicated that when pupils are provided with knowledge condensed in an infographic form, they are more likely to interact with the content.[3]

---

3.   Bicen, H. and Beheshti, M. (2017) 'The Psychological Impact of Infographics in Education'. Retrieved from: www.bit.ly/38ZvgGZ

When pupils create their own infographics, this can provide the right conditions for them to actively engage in both the construction of knowledge to be included, as well as the organisation of the infographic design, for it to then be used as a future tool for reflection. The combination of images and words, dual coding, supports the recall and recognition of the knowledge presented as outlined by Paivio's research at the beginning of the chapter. This designing process can provide the right conditions to enhance meaningful learning.

When applying it in the classroom, pupils could use infographics to present the following type of information:

1. In history, a timeline of the key events that led to world wars.
2. In geography, a step by step guide to explaining how to conduct a geographical fieldwork enquiry or outlining the sequence involved in the formation of physical landforms, like waterfalls and coastal stacks.
3. In science, an annotated chart to show the trends or changes over time in relation to Hess's Law when looking at enthalpy change.
4. In English, a focus on one character from *A Christmas Carol*.

In the following two spotlights, Rosemin and Kirsty share how they have implemented the 'C' of CRAFT in their classrooms.

Teacher Spotlight
Rosemin Guerrero Mitha, RE and psychology teacher at the Jumeirah English Speaking School in Dubai.

Teacher bio-sketch: Rosemin has been teaching for over ten years, qualifying in the UK having worked there for six years as the head of RE and psychology. She currently resides in Dubai working as a teacher of psychology and the Head of Wellbeing at Jumeirah English Speaking School (JESS). Rosemin has a passion for positive education and having been a middle leader in both academic and pastoral capacities, her philosophy of education advocates wellbeing at its forefront for all members of the school community. Rosemin is also a professional visual harvester. You can find her tweeting at @roseminguerrero

'ANYONE CAN DRAW!'

I love my subject – I mean, who doesn't? We should love the discipline that we teach because, as educators, one of the most important roles we play is instill-ing the love of learning of the subject we are teaching to those young people in front of us. As such, being a teacher of psychology, I have always aspired to teach valuable lessons beyond the syllabi we follow. Understanding behaviour and cognition is more than just theory and research, but it is experiencing it too. With a background in positive education and a fervent interest in the science of wellbeing, I endeavour to use elements of these two areas in the teaching and learning processes taking place in my classroom.

VISUAL HARVESTING

The term 'visual harvesting' is rarer than the use of terms such as graphic facilitation, graphic recording, and oftentimes, sketch noting. I prefer the use of visual Harvesting because, in my opinion, there is an organic essence to the name that the latter do not seem to capture and it is ultimately an organic process when in action. Furthermore, having briefly trained (by the KHDA) in 'visual harvesting' it is a term familiar to the educational institutions in Dubai.

INSTILLING CONFIDENCE

Visual harvesting is introduced to the class using a visual stimulus of animated rat with the affirmation 'anyone can cook' above it. The image is from the movie *Ratatouille* and Remy is the name of the rat. Remy is a rat in Paris who thrives on the words of Chef Gusteau whose motto is 'anyone can cook'. The movie is an inspiring tale of resilience and courage by the most unlikely of hero and this is the same inspiration with which I scaffold the learning and experience of visual harvesting in my classroom.

MODELLING

Students are shown examples of 'end products' such as my own and others' work. Their attention is drawn to the simple shapes and the organisation. Examples of 'live harvesting' are also shared for them to know that it is possible to create a harvest almost spontaneously. To do this, I start by asking them to visualise certain words (*i.e.* communication) then ask what communication would look like in an image. In one lesson students called out 'speech bubbles', 'jigsaws' and 'megaphone' and I showed them some basics such as drawing people with bodies (bean people or square people) with speech bubbles that are connected and that most icons are made up of simple shapes such as squares, circles, triangles and rectangles. But at this stage, I do not let them practice and just repeat the phrase that 'anyone can draw'.

INTRODUCE THE SUBJECT MATERIAL

In the lessons photographed, Year 10 students were halfway through a research in psychology unit and we had exhausted the topic experiments in a lot of detail with much written work and exam practice. With four remaining research methods still to study, each group was given the choice of one of the following: questionnaires, observations, case studies or interviews. With one A4 side of information and no prior learning, students were then asked to go ahead with harvesting the explanation of the research method including examples, plus the strengths and limitations of the method.

THE GROUND RULES:

- **Be bold** – Go big! Big icons on big paper, such as A1 flip chart paper.
- **Be brave** and draw in big marker pens, no pencil allowed even for practising.
- **Be colourful** for organisation and clarity.
- **Faith in yourself** because 'anyone can draw'.
- **Ten words only,** excluding the title.

The last piece of advice is that they visualise the words/concepts in their mind first, then verbalise what they see. Next, they think about how that translates into an icon. If they are not sure how to draw what they have visualised, they could practise on another sheet (still in pen) or Google the phrase 'how to draw/doodle communication easy', which brings up numerous images to aid them with translating what they have encoded visually onto paper.

    This introductory lesson to visual harvesting is always so satisfying to teach as it draws upon so many valuable areas of learning. Firstly, students engage in collaborative work (in pairs or threes) and it is challenging regardless of ability level and inclusive of any learning need. Secondly, there tends to be much fear initially, but they overcome this with risk-taking and bravery, which is beautiful to see. Lastly, and most importantly, they are learning. Once they are talking over how to depict the concepts and start drawing meaningfully, they are making the stick. This is facilitated by checking what they know by asking them to talk through the concepts without the information sheet. Most students can recite the information effortlessly and surprise themselves with how much they know. There is a 'feel-good' factor during these lessons, which is so conducive to a successful learning environment. Moreover, students develop a skill that we use time and time again in lessons and one that is transferable to any area of their learning. In a nutshell, visual harvesting synthesises and packages information effectively and continues to be a successful learning and revision tool in my classroom.

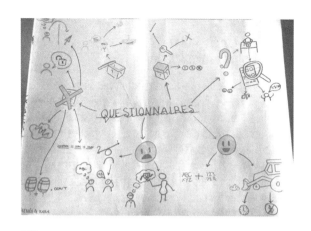

Teacher Spotlight
Kirsty Barker, Head of Dance at
Ormiston Bolingbroke Academy

Teacher bio-sketch: Kirsty has been teaching for ten years which has led on to a variety of roles. She led on the Creative Curriculum across Key Stage 3 consisting of project-based learning covering dance, drama and art. She then became Head of Dance and has been an active teaching and learning assistant across her teaching practice. Kirsty gained a master's degree in teaching and learning at the University of Chester, which then led her to become her academy's RQT & MA programme leader. She has been a moderator for the AQA GCSE dance and enjoys sharing best practice across other institutions. Kirsty has a passion for the arts and assisting teachers with their classroom practice.

Within dance, students need to recall a wide range of skills that they are able to use within practical lessons as well as in their written exam. It is a large volume of content they need to recall and so over my past ten years in the classroom I have found some of the following condensing methods to be the most successful.

MNEMONICS

To help my students store these key skills and vocabulary in their long-term memory I use mnemonics. If I was to list the physical skills, they must know within GCSE dance it can be overwhelming for them. Therefore, I have found that mnemonics are an effective way to break this down for them as well as being a useful tool to help with their recall.

The 'expressive skills' that we develop include:

- Musicality
- Communication of choreographic intent
- Facial expression
- Spatial awareness
- Sensitivity to other dancers
- Projection
- Phrasing and focus

By taking the first letter of each skill, we then, as a class, come up with a poem or phrase together to help them retain the information. I always put the ownership onto the students to come up with the poem so that it is them taking control of their own learning, rather than me dictate this to them.

I have found the more humorous the mnemonics are, the more likely the students are to retain them. As with any revision technique, this process needs to be completed at least three times over a period of time to be sustained within the student's long-term memory. Therefore, this needs to be revisited on numerous occasions to ensure the student holds onto the knowledge they have learnt.

ACTIONS/MOVEMENT SEQUENCES

Another way I like to condense information is by using actions/movement sequences. Having a passion for dance, it only makes sense for me to be able to remember information by putting it into a routine. Research has proven that dancing helps improve brain function and boosts memory (Machado, 2018).[4] Several studies have shown that dancing improves the cognitive domains and can boost your mood and reduce stress – a perfect reason to use this method with my students! I will create an action for each skill and place them into a movement sequence as outlined using physical skills in the stick men below.

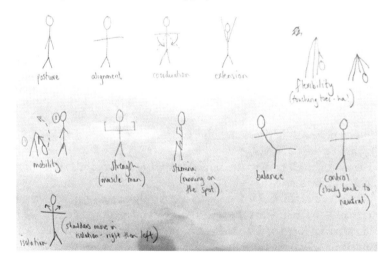

Again, these actions will be a collaborative process with the students so they take ownership of them and, therefore, I will just be the facilitator. They will then participate in performing the sequence as they say the skills out loud. Again, they will repeat the phrase over and over to commit this to their memory.

4. Teixeira-Machado L., Arida, R. M. and de Jesus Mari, J. (2019) 'Dance for neuroplasticity: A descriptive systematic review', *Neuroscience & Biobehavioral Reviews* 96 pp. 232-240.

They will then have to revisit this sequence at various stages across the term/year/course to ensure it transfers to their long-term memory. I find this is a great way to condense information if you have learners who are more creative and active learners as they find it a fun learning activity. It's a great way to test their knowledge at random points in a lesson or learning sequence by asking them to just stand up sporadically and perform it.

I shared this technique with colleagues during staff CPD sessions and it was trialled within some science lessons by the head of department. He asked students to use movement to show him how the planets orbit around the solar system. He took the entire class onto the yard and asked groups of students to represent the different planets orbiting around the solar system by giving them different pathways to travel along. He also introduced props so that the students were clearly identifiable to the others in the class. This got the students active in their learning and helped them when he later asked them in their learning, 'remember when we went on the yard that time…', and students were able to recall as it was a very different lesson to them writing in their books. He also used movement to get students to create waves and how they can travel by using their bodies to pass down energy in a line from one side of the classroom to the other. In his feedback to colleagues about trialling this technique, he was impressed by how well students were able to recall the information from that task later in the term.

Chapter review

- Pupils perceive that they are effectively revising by re-reading and high-lighting previous notes.
- The act of reading over the same information numerous times creates a feel-good factor.
- We want pupils to be able to generate powerful condensed notes of their own so that they can use them to revisit, review and reflect on knowledge learnt.
- The driving force of our intellectual performance is knowledge, which is stored in schematic form in long-term memory.
- Our working memory is fragile and limited, when it is required to process too much information this can cause cognitive overload.

Chapter reflections

The way in which teachers CRAFT their delivery of the complex concepts and processes that characterise our subjects is important to enable them to use this knowledge to condense learning. If we want pupils to be effective learners, we need to support them in creating powerful knowledge notes that allow them to use these to reflect and retrieve learning over time to build schemas and strengthen long-term memory. In the next chapter, we will explore how teachers can support pupils in become reflective learners in the 'R' of CRAFT.

THE 'R': HOW DO WE GENERATE REFLECTIVE LEARNERS?

OLIVER CAVIGLIOLI
@olicav olicav.com

'To reflect: to think deeply or carefully about something.'

Sarah, an English teacher of three years, has spent the last six weeks teaching Year 11 about A Christmas Carol, exploring the content and context. She has worked tirelessly to delve into the meaning of the novella. Pupils have made detailed annotations, demonstrating what appeared to be a good understanding of the text. However, three weeks later when it comes to their assessment, pupils' performance doesn't reflect their classwork. Sarah is confused. She was certain she had 'taught' the novella and pupils had demonstrated understanding in the lesson, therefore, she believed they should have performed better in their assessment.

During the early stages of my career it was all about discovery-based learning. Whole-school CPD focused on the concept that if teachers created memorable learning experiences for students, they would remember what they had been taught. I recall on several occasions being observed as a 'facilitator' in the room, with one lesson involving students working together to understand the processes that occurred at the different tectonic plate margins. The students would carousel around the room, gathering information; they were on a plate tectonic mission. The lesson didn't involve much input from me. There was little teacher talk as pupils discovered the complex processes that took place by themselves. The room was buzzing with noise and activity; the pupils were working well, or so it would have seemed. Just like in the example of Sarah's English lesson, I believed that because I had provided the means for the pupils to discover the content through the activity and students had appeared to perform well in the lesson, learning had taken place. It was only when it came to a form of assessment a few weeks later that it was as if the lesson hadn't taken place. Pupils couldn't recall the key concepts and processes they had been discovering so their explanations of the processes at the plate tectonic margins were littered with errors and misconceptions. When I asked them if they could recall the lesson, the responses were, 'Oh yes, was that the lesson when we were plate tectonic detectives, sir?' Others would respond with, 'I really enjoyed that lesson, can we do something like that again, sir?'

Fast-forward to today and the evidence-based research from cognitive scientists have highlighted the problem that many teachers like Sarah and I were experiencing. Whilst I had provided the means for them to acquire knowledge and believed that it would 'stick', they hadn't retained the knowledge, or even understood it, therefore they hadn't learnt it.

When deliberating over the reasons why, even though we have taught the lesson pupils appear to not have learnt what was taught, the work of Paul A. Kirschner, John Sweller and Richard E. Clark provides a useful and widely accepted definition: 'Learning is defined as an alteration in long-term memory.'[1]

In the example of the plate tectonic lesson, the pupils had predominantly remembered the 'task' they were doing – the mission – however the knowledge hadn't stuck. The lesson was memorable but for all the wrong reasons. This is where, as teachers, our understanding of how memory works when we are considering how to generate truly reflective learners is crucial. Tulving's research indicated humans possess two forms of memory, episodic and semantic, which work in different ways to transfer information we receive. Episodic memory is essentially an autobiographic account of our life – it takes little to no effort, for example, 'we were on a mission', 'we did a carousel', or 'there were builders making a noise during our geography lesson'. These are all the personal experiences that the students remembered related to that lesson. When I ask my daughter

1.   Kirschner, P. A., Sweller, J. and Clark, R. E. (2006) 'Why Minimal Guidance During Instruction Does Not Work: An Analysis of the Failure of Constructivist, Discovery, Problem-Based, Experiential, and Inquiry-Based Teaching', Educational Psychologist 41 (2) pp. 75-86.

what she did at school, she will often recall events that took place in the lesson, rather than the knowledge acquired. When I probe her about the knowledge, this requires her to think harder to recall what she was studying in a specific lesson. Therefore, there is disconnect between the information pupils receive and the experience, with the latter often the more memorable. This makes episodic memory rigid to that episode, reducing its transferability to different contexts. In contrast, semantic memory is an organised system of information – language, symbols, formulas, concepts and facts – related to what we study. For example, knowing the different dates of key historical events, the processes of erosion, or the formula to working out the diameter of a circle. This form of memory is separated from any emotion, timeline, or spatial context. It is flexible, and once information is stored in the semantic memory, we can transfer it to different contexts, which makes it key to supporting learning. However, the retention of our semantic memories can deteriorate over time and it is the strengthening of these memories that is important to improving retention and knowledge recall.

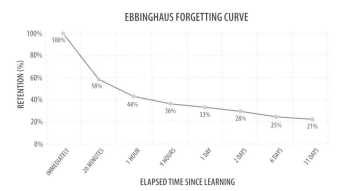

The work of German psychologist Herman Ebbinghaus illustrates how, over time, the human brain can lose information learnt and subsequently stored in our semantic memory. This led to what Ebbinghaus coined the forgetting curve, which illustrated the deterioration of acquired information over time. However, the work of Ebbinghaus has been criticised because his research was based on his ability to recall a list of words by listening and repeating them over and over until he was able to remember them. To test the validity of Ebbinghaus' study other scientists have replicated it, yielding similar results to the original study. In one replicated study, the ten lists of words were learnt and relearnt for the same time-intervals of 20 minutes, after 1 hour, 9 hours, 1 day, 2 days, 6 days and 31 days. The results generated by the replicated study demonstrated a very similar curve to that of Ebbinghaus, where over a 75-day period there was an average increase in the learning time of 2.67 seconds per day.[2]

What is clear from Ebbinghaus and others who have replicated his original study is the ability to recall information from memory decreases over time from its initial point of exposure. The study by Roediger and Karpicke (2006), illustrated by the graph below, produced results supporting the use of repeated retrieval practice. Where the participants merely repeatedly studied items, it produced no effect on retention compared to the other participants who used repeated retrieval. In the study conducted, the repeated retrieval produced a 150% improvement in long-term retention.

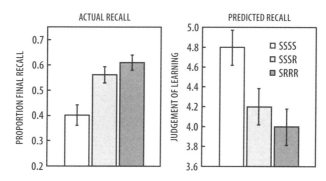

This begins to offer some explanations as to why teachers have become frustrated and deflated in recent years when, despite all efforts to create meaningful learning experiences, pupils often deny any knowledge of the previous lessons taking place. This has become an ever-increasing challenge with the revised GCSE specifications because pupils are expected to recall knowledge at the end of a two-year course, or in the case of many secondary schools up and down the country, recalling knowledge at the end of a three-year course.

The rate at which we forget information varies dependent on our prior knowledge, the way in which the knowledge was presented and to some extent our motivation to receive the information. Consequently, if we are to improve pupils' efficiency in learning, we must provide opportunities for them to reflect. In the words of Andrew C. Butler and Henry L. Roediger: 'The critical mechanism for promoting retention of information is the successful retrieval of that information.'

2.   Murre, J. M. J. and Dros, J. (2015) 'Replication and Analysis of Ebbinghaus' Forgetting Curve', PLoS ONE 10 (7). Retrieved from: www.bit.ly/38v1xWa

If we know that our retention of knowledge deteriorates over time, and that as teachers we must provide opportunities for pupils to practise retrieving information, we need to understand what I believe is the 'optimal retrieval gap'. This is the time gap between pupils encoding new information and then retrieving it, also commonly referred to as 'spaced practice'. The image below represents an example of the retrieval gap that teachers should consider when planning for pupils to recall previously encoded concepts and processes.

Below is a diagrammatic representation of the encoding and retrieval of material by Ben Ranson.

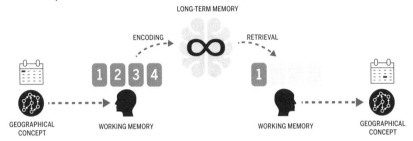

Typically, we check for pupils' understanding during and/or at the end of a lesson, however the information pupils have received at this point in the lesson is likely to still be in their working memory. Therefore, we need to carefully plan the time between when new material is learnt and reviewed. But, how can we as teachers embed an 'optimum retrieval gap' during the current and previous academic year?

When it comes to pupils preparing for an internal assessment or for a terminal examination at the end of Key Stage 4 and 5, many pupils believe that cramming their revision will be an effective approach to preparing for these assessments. This is a not an effective approach to improving memory. The benefits of spaced practice or rehearsal were first suggested by Ebbinghaus following his forgetting curve experiment. He identified that when he spaced out repetitions of recalling the series of 12 syllables over a three-day period, he could almost halve the number of repetitions necessary. He concluded that, **'a suitable distribution of (repetitions) over a space of time is decidedly more advantageous than the massing of them at a single time.'**[3] Since Ebbinghaus' research, other scientists have conducted similar studies to explore the benefits of spacing recall compared with massed practice. Subsequent studies demonstrated the positive impact of this approach in improving longer-term retention of knowledge.

---

3. Weinstein, Y., Madan, C. R. and Sumeracki, M. A. (2018) 'Teaching the science of learning', Cognitive Research: Principles and Implications 3 (article no. 2).

Bjork's theory of disuse provides an explanation of the benefits of spacing learning, indicating that the memories we encode have both a retrieval and storage strength. For example, pupils will often mention to me after an assessment that they revised for it and thought they knew the concepts and processes, but when completing the assessment, they say their minds went blank. When reviewing their assessment during the feedback process, it is also a regular response from many pupils when they say, 'Oh yes, of course I knew it was that!' This is because the process of cramming information in a short space of time will cause the information to be lost at a faster rate due to it consisting of a high retrieval strength and low storage strength. Bjork's theory suggests that retrieval strength is believed to indicate the ease of which a memory can be recalled, whereas storage strength represents the extent to which a memory has been encoded into our mind. To demonstrate, when something is well learnt – for example, your mobile number – it has a high retrieval and storage strength. You know it well and can easily recall it when required to do so. In comparison, when buying a new house, the postcode of your new address may have a high retrieval strength but a low storage strength. When it comes to the classroom environment information that students receive throughout their five-hour lessons can have a low retrieval and low storage strength. When teachers demonstrate to pupils how to space their learning repeatedly over a set period rather than cramming the strength of learning can be improved. This can be challenging though because the act of retrieving and spacing their learning from memory is difficult, but it is this increased challenge of retrieving effort that will improve the durability of what is being learnt, something Bjork termed as 'desirable difficulties'.

The combination of retrieval and spaced practice can be powerful in strengthening pupils' long-term memory, which in turn will create the conditions for effective learning. However, it is important that as teachers we see the use of retrieval practice as a learning strategy and not as an assessment tool to be used to measure or grade a pupil. We want to create these episodes of 'desirable difficulties' for pupils to see the benefits to their long-term retention. The implementation of regular retrieval practice to review information from memory, with low or no-stakes, has demonstrated it can contribute towards reducing the anxiety that many pupils have towards taking a test. Cognitive scientists have indicated the negative impact that induced stress can have on impairing memory retrieval. In one experiment, one group of participants were provided with information to be learnt by restudying, while another group were provided with information to be learnt by retrieval practice. After the first 24 hours, the group that conducted the restudying of information were given induced stress. The results demonstrated the restudy group experienced stress-related impairment in comparison to the retrieval practice group who appeared immune to the effects of stress.[4] Therefore, the research suggests that the more pupils engage in the process of retrieval, the more pupils see the benefits of this process because it will lead to an increase in confidence about the reviewing of information.

Retrieval practice, or the use of low- or no-stakes quizzes in the classroom, can be implemented school-wide without increasing students' self-reported test anxiety. In fact, frequent quizzing seems to alleviate test anxiety.[5]

The challenge for teachers is how to apply this evidence-based research in the day-to-day classroom. I regularly share with my pupils the example of an actor rehearsing a script to deliver a play or an athlete training for an event. These people wouldn't leave it until the last minute before going on the stage; they will prepare and practise over time. I find using examples of some of their idols helps to support this concept and pupils can then relate to the reasons why regular reviewing of their learning spaced out over time will be more beneficial than cramming. In the research conducted, there is no specific guidelines on the time we should suggest to our pupils to review something they have learnt, however the research indicates that the most beneficial time to recall information is at the point when we're about to forget it. This is because the more difficult the retrieval activity, the greater the benefit this will have on strengthening our long-term memory. This time will be dependent on each individual pupil and the information they are remembering. A more effective approach to advocate to our pupils is short bursts of retrieval every day of 30 minutes to an hour that will be more beneficial than one long seven-hour session.

So, what strategies can teachers use to generate reflective learners? In *Teach Like Nobody's Watching*, Mark Enser suggests that teachers can build lessons around four key elements: recap, input, application and feedback. The beginning of the lesson is an ideal opportunity to capitalise on recapping from previous lessons with pupils' recalling information from their long-term memory to their working memory. It is also two of the ten principles that Barak Rosenshine indicates expert teachers do in his 'Principles of Instruction' paper:

---

4. Wolf, O. T. and Kluge, A. (2017) 'Commentary: Retrieval practice protects memory against acute stress', Frontiers in Behavioral Neuroscience 11 (48).
5. Agarwal, P. K., D'Antonio, L., Roediger III, H. L., McDermott, K. B. and McDaniel, M. A. (2014) 'Classroom-based programs of retrieval practice reduce middle school and high school students' test anxiety', Journal of Applied Research in Memory and Cognition 3 (3) pp. 131-139.

1. **Begin a lesson with a short review of previous learning: daily review can strengthen previous learning and can lead to fluent recall.** Rosenshine highlights from the research that the most effective teachers began their lesson with a five to eight-minute review of previously covered material. Teachers use this review time to reflect on vocabulary, formulae, events or previously learnt concepts.
2. **Engage students in weekly and monthly review. Students need to be involved in extensive practice in order to develop well-connected and automatic knowledge.** In his paper, Rosenshine indicates that expert teachers create regular opportunities for pupils to rehearse and review information and, in time, improve learning by recalling information with increased automaticity.[6]

Whilst Rosenshine believed recapping previous learning was important in strengthening the material already learnt, it is also an ideal point in the lesson where teachers can review the concepts and processes that will be relevant for the coming lesson. This not only allows the teacher to assess prior knowledge before teaching the new material, it also allows for pupils to free up their working memory to enable space to receive and encode new material. If pupils must work hard to recall previously learnt material whilst learning new material, this can make it difficult for the new material to be received and encoded correctly.

So far in this chapter we have considered the benefit of teachers using research-based evidence to generate reflective learners. The next section of this chapter will explore a range of strategies that all teachers could apply in their classroom to support pupils in developing their resilience at regularly retrieving knowledge from memory, both in and out of the classroom.

Strategy 1: Low-stake spaced quizzing

Begin the lesson with six low-stake questions where students are expected to actively recall information from their long-term memory to their working memory, without any aid from previous notes or peers. Generate questions that allow for retrieval of concepts and processes over time, for example: two questions from last week, two from last term, and two from last year, creating opportunities for students to think hard and recall knowledge over a longer time. The low-stake nature of these questions means you can provide instant

6.   Rosenshine, B. (2012) 'Principles of Instruction', *American Educator* [Online] Spring 2012 . Retrieved from: www.bit.ly/3cBJfWA

feedback following the quiz and use the evidence to inform future planning, or explicitly re-teach a concept or process at that point before moving on. As discussed earlier in this chapter, it is important to create a culture whereby all pupils regularly reflecting on their learning where they understand there is no or low stakes.

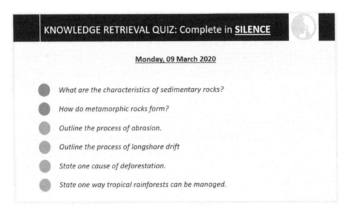

One of the key factors in generating reflective learners is for them to understand the importance of the science behind how we learn. Sharing this with your pupils can be a powerful tool to raise their awareness of how they can become more reflective learners. Whilst writing this book, I asked several pupils their thoughts of retrieving knowledge from memory using this type of quiz.

'I believe that having a quiz at the start of a lesson allows me to recap knowledge. They allow me to challenge my memory from past lessons and boost my overall knowledge of key information and facts. Without these short quizzes, I don't think I would remember as many facts.' – Emily, a Year 10 student.

'In my opinion, having an opportunity to recall knowledge leads you to memorise and understand subjects/topics a lot more because you are constantly recapping your knowledge. For example, at the beginning of Year 7 I got confused by the different processes of erosion. I can now remember what they are and what they mean. I believe that they are very effective.' – Eva, a Year 9 student.

The process of retrieving information doesn't have to be a quiz at the start of the lesson; it could be done through a range of other activities, at any point in a lesson. In fact, the use of retrieval practice in supporting students to reflect on their learning involves minimal preparation by teachers but should require maximum effort by pupils. Here are some other examples of strategies that teachers can use to support students in conducting retrieval practice, which could be used by pupils both inside and outside of the classroom.

Strategy 2: Memory dump

This is an opportunity for pupils to recall knowledge about a concept or process, which could be completed simply by using a blank sheet of paper. For example, giving pupils five minutes to recall the physical and human causes of river flooding, or the events that led to World War I. Just like the retrieval quiz, this should be done independently from memory and without any notes. Once the time is up, instant feedback can be provided through peer discussion around what they have managed to recall. Then using a knowledge organiser, they can identify the gaps in knowledge, and this can become a focus for their homework during that week, or again if there is a concept or process that needs explicitly re-teaching, this might be the ideal opportunity to do this before moving on.

Strategy 3: Memory draw

In Chapter 1, we explored the benefits of drawing to condense knowledge and create powerful learning notes. A quick retrieval practice exercise is to get pupils to draw from memory. For example, when looking at the processes of weathering, students draw the process before writing their understanding of it. This is a quick, low stake activity to encourage pupils to bring information back to mind through drawing out the concept or process prior to discussing their recall with the teacher or their peers. In religious education this activity could be used when Key Stage 2 teachers are reviewing pupils understanding of what Christians believe.

Strategy 4: Image recall

The use of images in lesson is a powerful strategy in supporting knowledge recall and retention, which can be done in several ways to support the strengthening of long-term memory and in turn, learning. For example, in science when teachers are exploring the features of animal and plant cells, students are presented with a non-labelled diagram and asked to annotate the image to recall the key features. After attempting to recall the key features of the animal and plant cells, teachers can provide instant feedback.

ANIMAL CELL   PLANT CELL

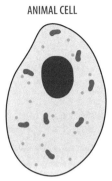 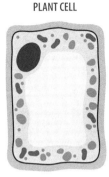

Another example for the use of images to retrieve information is in physical education when pupils are reviewing their understanding of the muscular system. This could be reviewed in the lesson by providing pupils with an image of the main muscles in the human body. The task is then for pupils to use the image to support the recall of the location of the hip flexors, quadriceps, biceps and quadriceps.

Strategy 5: Vocab race

Recalling the range of vocabulary in subjects is vital for pupils to have a clear understanding of the subject language that they will have to apply to different contexts. For example, in GCSE dance when developing their understanding of performance skills, pupils would need to know examples of physical skills, recognise how they would be demonstrated in a performance, and how to develop their own use of the skill and how to improve it in their own performances. This could be done as a verbal retrieval activity with pupils recalling the meaning of the subject vocabulary with their peers, or through the teacher choosing a key term, and pupils demonstrating the meaning to the teacher.

Physical Skills	Alignment	Balance	Coordination
Control	Flexibility	Mobility	Strength
Stamina	Extension	Isolation	Posture

Another example of how to utilise a vocab race is in Spanish when pupils are developing their written and spoken language related to phrases and vocabulary associated with different types of houses and home life. Pupils are given a set time to recall the phrases and vocabulary from memory before sharing these with peers and the teacher.

My home	el comedor	el dormitorio	el vestibulo
la habitacion	el garaje	el salon	el jardin

Strategy 6: Reverse retrieval

This strategy involves pupils working backwards to retrieve the factors or components of a concept or process they have previously studied. In the science example below, pupils have been studying how bacteria can be genetically engineered to produce insulin, which can then be easily extracted for use in the pharmaceutical industry. Pupils would work to recall the prior knowledge needed to get to the end point in this knowledge sequence. For example, in the middle box pupils would be expected to recall the steps associated with genetic engineering, including the enzymes required for the process. Then the first box would be the starting point. This would be the recall of eukaryotic and prokaryotic organelles. Similarly, in geography, when pupils are studying the interaction of physical processes in the formation of river, coastal and glacial landforms, the teacher provides an image of the landform in the furthest right box. Pupils then recall the different stages in the formation of the landform.

Strategy 7: Retrieval ripple

A retrieval ripple is an ideal activity to use with pupils when considering how different factors link together. For example, when pupils are developing a knowledge schema on the causes of World War II, pupils try to recall from memory the different factors that led to triggering the war. The ripple provides a structure for pupils to consider how one event can lead to another event, and so on. In English, when pupils are exploring the influence of Mrs Johnstone in Blood Brothers, they consider her behaviour, interactions, personality and beliefs and how this impacts on the actions she takes during the play. For example, her superstitious belief and how Mrs Lyons manipulates this to convince Mrs Johnstone to give her baby away. Pupils may use quotes in their retrieval ripple to demonstrate how this is shown in the play, such as, 'you never put new shoes on the table'. Pupils would then explore further examples and then could use a further ripple on the writer's intentions.

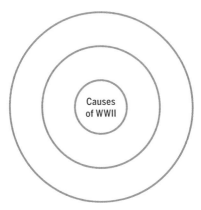

Strategy 8: Learning journey/personalised learning checklists

When considering how to generate reflective learners this is a key strategy that all teachers can use with their pupils. If we want pupils to reflect on their learning over time to reduce forgetting and improve memory strength, we need to provide a clear overview of the curriculum journey. Following the retrieval quiz, I usually start the lesson with something like:

- 'Do you remember last lesson when we…?'
- 'Well, today we are going to build on that knowledge to…'
- 'By gaining an understanding of… we will be able to…'

I want students to be immersed in their learning journey and know how the different threads of their curriculum tapestry are weaved together. Alongside this, provide a road map indicating the key questions that pupils will be able to answer by the end of a topic. The example below is a road map illustrating the big questions pupils will explore for a Year 7 geography unit on distinctive landscapes. As well as the road maps, personalised learning checklists are a useful tool to signpost to pupils the core knowledge that will underpin the unit. I will often ask pupils to reflect on the core knowledge at the start of the unit to determine their prior knowledge and bring back to mind some of their previous schema from other units that link to this new unit. This is also a great activity to make the links between units explicit to pupils, developing their understanding of how different webs of knowledge connect.

Strategy 9: The Leitner System

The Leitner System was devised by Austrian Sebastian Leitner. It is a spaced repetition system using flashcards to improve learning. As discussed in Chapter 1, it is important pupils create flashcards that have the core concept or process on one side and the required knowledge relating to that concept or process on the opposite side. For example, a process of erosion that acts on coastal landscapes is abrasion. This would be written on the front of the flashcard and the definition of the process on the opposite side. Once pupils have condensed their notes to create a set of flashcards, we can teach them to use the Leitner System to reflect on their ability to recall information. Leitner conducted a series of experiments using a box to store his flashcards, which contained several compartments. He placed new flashcards in the first compartment, and he reviewed these flashcards every day. When he was able to answer the flashcard correctly, he moved this to the second compartment and set the repetition retrieval to two days. Then any answered correctly were moved into the third compartment. If pupils adopt the Leitner System when using flashcards to reflect on learning, this will help pupils to understand what information they know well and focus study on information that they don't know as well.

When sharing the Leitner System with your pupils try the following guidance to support them:

1. Create a minimum of five boxes to place flashcards in with the following timelines marked on them. Box 1 (everyday), box 2 (every two days), box 3 (every five days), box 4 (every ten days) and box 5 (every 15 days).
2. Every card starts in the first box.
3. When knowledge on a flashcard is correctly recalled, move this card into the next box on the right.
4. When knowledge isn't correctly recalled, move this flashcard to the left.

CORRECTLY ANSWERED CARDS

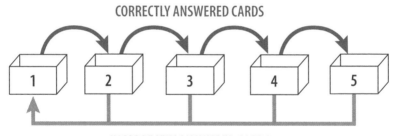

INCORRECTLY ANSWERED CARDS

Strategy 10: Homework

For many years I have trialled different approaches to homework to create meaningful opportunities outside of the classroom. In many cases, it involved students completing an unfinished task, or applying their knowledge to exam-style questions. It soon became a cycle of chasing students for incomplete homework and an unmanageable workload for marking, and more importantly, providing feedback. Something had to change! This change was a shift in the focus of homework to students condensing learning as discussed in Chapter 1 and reflecting on the learning from the week. It is important that we provide pupils with the opportunity to engage in reflecting on their learning outside of the classroom on a weekly and monthly basis to strengthen and improve the fluency in knowledge recall that we have explored in this chapter. When pupils engage in regular homework, they perform better in subsequent assessments compared with those pupils who don't.

There are now several online homework platforms that teachers can use to set up reflection homework activities for pupils on a weekly basis. For example, Seneca Learning provides homework for a range of subjects across the key stages using smart learning algorithms to support pupils in remembering concepts and processes. When pupils get a question wrong, they will be re-exposed to the content again during the module but in a different way. The benefit of using an online learning platform like Seneca is it sets the optimal gap for when the content should be revisited based on their performance when answering the questions. This is a great way for pupils to engage in a weekly and monthly review of information previously learnt and automatically indicates pupil's performance against the knowledge strands, which allows teachers to utilise these insights in their own classroom weekly and monthly reviews.

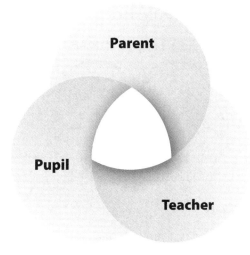

Strategy 11: Engaging parents

When considering how to generate more reflective learners there is one element that we haven't discussed in this chapter so far – parental engagement. Parental involvement is a key cog in the 'R' of CRAFT.

This engagement with parents will require a whole-school drive to provide the triangulation between school and home to contribute towards improving pupils' understanding and retention of information received in lessons. The following are several examples that teachers can imbed to support this triangulation.

- Share the learning journey for the term and the academic year with parents. This will allow them to understand the knowledge pupils will be learning and how this fits together in an overall sequence.
- Create opportunities at parents evening to demonstrate to parents the most effective strategies to support their child in reviewing information learnt from the previous week, month and year.
- Allow pupils to take their class notes home on a half-termly basis and encourage them to engage in a dialogue about the knowledge they have learnt. Provide a review sticker, like the one below originally created by Kate Stockings, for parents to acknowledge this conversation and make a comment. This will cultivate the opportunities for pupils and parents to be involved and open a dialogue about their learning journey in your subject. It is also a useful strategy, if completed termly and before a parents evening, to create a more focused exchange when discussing their child's progress.

Geography Parent/Carer Book Review Autumn Term 2018	
Comments on classwork, homework and overall presentation of book.	
Signed: Date:	

Strategy 12: Bug twist

The BUG strategy (**box** the command word, **underline** the key words, **glance** back at the question) is a well-known technique to support pupils when applying knowledge to examination style questions. It can help in ensuring pupils don't just write 'everything they know' about a concept or process that doesn't directly answer the question set. A possible alternative to the traditional BUG strategy is to remove the command word and key words for pupils to recall with prompts. This could be adapted to be used at the start of a lesson or prior to pupils applying knowledge.

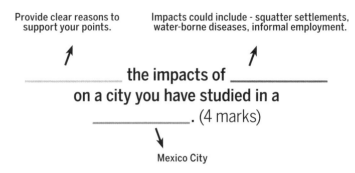

Provide clear reasons to support your points.

Impacts could include - squatter settlements, water-borne diseases, informal employment.

the impacts of _____ on a city you have studied in a _____. (4 marks)

Mexico City

In the following two teacher spotlights, Ben Ranson and Flavia S. Belham share how they have supported pupils in becoming more reflective learners.

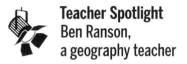

Teacher Spotlight
Ben Ranson,
a geography teacher

Teacher bio-sketch: Ben has taught geography in the UK and China, serving as a classroom teacher, head of department and senior leader. An attempted researcher, Ben dropped out of his postgraduate studies after spending four years trying to finalise his thoughts and findings on ideological bias in development narratives. Sipping on good coffee, he reads what brighter minds have to say about teaching, knowledge and the curriculum. He currently lives in Oxfordshire with his wife Jen, training for ultra-marathons with his dog, Hamish. You can find him tweeting at @ThatBenRanson

It's not an uncommon problem. Fellow teachers confided in me that we were all in the same boat. A light shower seemed all that was needed to wash away everything I thought my students had learnt from the previous lesson. My stomach turned uneasily with the thought of what this meant for them in the long term.

I made a strong coffee. No sugar, no milk. I read. The last sip was lukewarm by the time I was finished. I had, at last, a way forward. A route so simple that I felt at once stupid for not thinking of it before, and embarrassed to say aloud because, surely, everyone already knew.

As the stoics wrote, we are what we do every day. If I wanted my students to be better at remembering things, then we needed to practice being good at remembering things.

We started slow. Five questions on the interactive whiteboard as students walked in. Why five? Font size. I wanted to fit the questions and answers on the same slide. I wanted them bold. Five questions became the starter. Early results were poor; this was a new type of challenge. I focused on closed questions with a definitively correct answer, we could swap from the regular black or blue to a red pen, gracing the page with a quick tick or adding a correction.

The more often a question came up, the more frequently students got it right. So far, so obvious. Practice makes perfect. I upped the ante. Reduced the font. Eight questions. Ten. Still closed. Still self-marked in red. It got faster.

'I only got seven of them right', he said, a disappointing shrug in the direction of the three red-penned corrections on the page in front him matched his tone. We flicked back. A couple of weeks, further, a couple of months. 'Have a look here, how many were you getting right back in November?' Proof of progress from someone we might have once described as disaffected.

I caved first. Every lesson started the same. The dull pressure of self-doubt gnawed at me. Should every lesson start the same? I couldn't shake the sense that the sameness revealed some failing on my part. Long since conditioned in the art of the engaging starter, the routine of our retrieval practice began to feel like a betrayal.

I returned to the books, blogs and notes that I'd made. Each caffeine-fuelled page flick reassured me. This was the way. But, importantly, it didn't always need to feel the same. Definitive answers to closed questions aren't the only things we can remember, though they are the most reliable place to start.

I'd been reading a lot about vocabulary, a necessary side effect of being timetabled a few more lessons of English. I was interested in the sentence structure building blocks outlined by the authors of *The Writing Revolution*. Subordinating conjunctions and appositive clauses took me in exciting new directions. A fusion of curriculum-driven cognitive heavy lifting retrieved later through developing students' skill in sentence structure.

Chronological conjunctions, sentences starting with before, after and when, required students to not only recall the components of sequences and processes but to do so in order. Appositive clauses, where the clause gives additional information related to the noun at the start of the sentence, freed students from the sameness I'd begun to fear. This felt like retrieval practice jacked-up on steroids, a heady rush, huge gains, but not free of consequence.

With no definitively correct answer, the ease of quick ticks and corrective comments was lost. Writing out sentences in exercise books, questions from students about what 'was' or 'wasn't' right ground the lessons to a halt. Sluggishly we slaved over our writing. I was in desperate need of some slickness.

Enter the mini whiteboard. Salvation. Speed returned. Students could join me in seeing the range of responses. Appetites were voracious when I offered the opportunity for peer assessment in small teams. Asking students to nominate the best sentence they could see in the classroom showcased provided the opportunity to hear students talk about syntax as well as the retrieved knowledge.

It's hard to imagine going back on starting every lesson with a reflection on what we already know. It's taken me from being in fear of a light shower to feeling equipped for a thunderstorm.

Teacher Spotlight
Dr Flavia Belham,
Chief Scientist at Seneca Learning

Teacher bio-sketch: Dr Flavia Belham is the Chief Scientist at Seneca Learning, applying experimental findings from Neuroscience to the platform's methodology. She is a certified teacher and has worked as a science/biology teacher in schools in the past. During her PhD in Cognitive Neuroscience at University College London (UCL), she used brain-imaging techniques to investigate how people of different ages memorise emotional events. You can find her tweeting at @FlaviaBelhamPhD

Over their years in school, students will learn a lot of content from a lot of different subjects. Some of this content will be seen as easy and enjoyable, some will be seen as complex and stressful. To help students learn as well as possible, one valuable technique is to condense information into memorable chunks.

An obvious example of this technique is in remembering long numbers. Imagine you need to remember the following digits in the exact order they are presented: 200619171568. It is much harder to remember them if you think of each digit individually. However, if you chunk this long number into three bits of four digits each, you get 2006, 1917, 1568. It is much easier to remember the information like that because now you have only three things to remember, instead of the original 12.

What about actual school content? How can it be condensed? What would that look like?

Here at Seneca, one of the first things we decided about our platform's methodology was that we would not have long videos or long texts. Rather, we chose to present information in quick and short summaries, which would be organised in bullet points and accompanied by a relevant image. With that, we intended to help students to focus on the core information, instead of on the peripheral content that unavoidably comes with a long text.

In addition to condensing the information into more memorable chunks, the Seneca platform restructures that information in new formats, including mind-maps, diagrams, lists, timelines, flashcards and even gifs. The idea here is that students can go from the really long notes they have accumulated over the years to a more straight-to-the-point knowledge that can then be used to rehearse and practice.

The way I like to explain the importance of condensing information and re-structuring it into different formats is with the analogy of a maze. Imagine that the entrance of the maze is an exam question and the exit is the correct answer. If students are always learning the same content in the same format, there is only one path they can take to go from the entrance to the exit of the maze. However, when they can transform their learning into new material, new paths become available and it is much easier to leave the maze successfully. Similarly, by removing the information that is not at the core of that content, they are also removing the dead ends of the maze, making much easier to find the exit.

Another advantage of showing content in different formats at Seneca is that we can display different case studies and examples. At a conference earlier this year, one teacher told me their students had not answered a question about how giraffes breathe because they had 'only learnt about how zebras breathe'. This means that they were not able to understand what is common of all mammals and what is unique of each species. At our Seneca platform, we like to ask the same question several times, but each time taking a different example as the basis. Again, this helps students to separate the core knowledge from the rest.

The feedback we have gotten from our 2.5 million students, teachers and parents say that this methodology is working very well. And the best thing is that our way of condensing connects perfectly with our way of helping students reflect.

For example, see our material on 'The Model of the Atom', for a GCSE course. We start by presenting the key information about each model in condensed, clear, objective and straightforward text.

 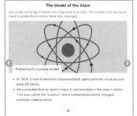 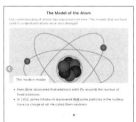

Then, part of the information is presented again in different formats, such as a mind map. You can say it has been re-condensed.

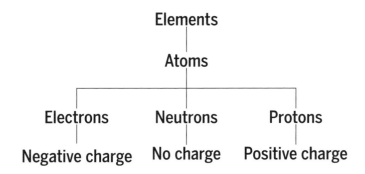

Following that, the main part of our methodology is to keep re-presenting the core knowledge in different formats, while simultaneously testing students in low-stake quizzes. See the examples:

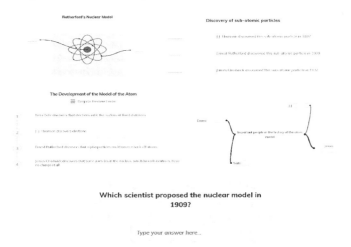

In conclusion, condensing is a very important learning strategy that helps students to restructure their knowledge, to identify the core content, to understand the commonalities and differences between cases, and to do retrieval practice as well. What we have learnt at Seneca is that a digital tool can scale that to millions of topics and people.

Chapter review

- For something to have been learnt it needs to be changed in our long-term memory.
- Humans possess two forms of memory, episodic and semantic, which work in different ways to transfer the information we receive.
- Semantic memories can deteriorate over time and it is the strengthening of these memories that are important to improving retention and knowledge recall.
- The ability to recall information from memory decreases over time from its initial point of exposure.
- When it comes to planning learning sequences, we should provide opportunities for pupils to practise retrieving information.
- When teachers demonstrate to pupils how to space their learning repeatedly over a set period rather than cramming, the strength of learning will be improved.
- The most beneficial time to recall information is at the point when we're about to forget it.
- Engaging parents is a key factor in the supporting the triangulation between school and home to improve pupils' understanding and retention of knowledge.

Chapter reflections

The research around knowledge retrieval and spaced practice provide strong evidence to support the effectiveness of these strategies in enhancing learning. When pupils are asked to engage in the process of retrieval and guided to space this over a period of time, rather than on mass, it produces direct effects on learning because every time we retrieve knowledge, that knowledge is altered and the ability to reconstruct that knowledge again in the future is enhanced. Therefore, to create truly reflective learners, we should cultivate opportunities in and out of the classroom where the maintenance of memory strength is supported through the regular access to knowledge in memory.

After considering how teachers can generate reflective learners, it's now time to explore how teachers can use a blend of formative and summative assessment, the A of CRAFT.

THE 'A': HOW CAN ASSESSMENT BE USED AS A RESPONSIVE TEACHING TOOL?

OLIVER CAVIGLIOLI
@olicav olicav.com

'If the purpose for learning is to score well on a test, we've lost sight of the real reason for learning.' – Jeannie Fulbright

Carl, a geography teacher of 20 years, spent many hours creating end of unit assessments to review his pupils' performance following a sequence of lessons. Once his classes had finished the assessment, he would record the level or grade that each individual pupil had achieved. Pupils would mark their scores on flight paths on the front of their exercise books throughout the academic year. It was a case of teaching content, set an assessment, mark it, give a level and then move on. These levels would then be uploaded at the request of school leaders to fulfil the data drop requirements at a whole-school level. Most of his pupils would achieve their expected level or in many cases exceed their target level for the end of year and move up their projected flight path, mapping this on the front of their exercise books. Happy days, or so Carl believed.

My views on how teachers assess pupils and how senior leaders implement whole-school assessment to track pupil progress have changed significantly, influenced by my other role in education as a principal examiner. For years

I spent hours creating assessments, usually at the end of a scheme of work or, even worse, I would retrospectively fit an assessment in to coincide with whole-school data drop requests. I remember trying to apply a 'best fit' approach to the pupil's assessment, using descriptors based on the national curriculum levels, which were by their very nature far too generic and difficult for a teacher to interpret. An extract of what I remember using in my first teaching post to interpret the difference between a Level 4 and Level 5 pupil in geography is illustrated below.

> Level 4: Pupils show knowledge and understanding of aspects of the geography of the UK and the wider world. They recognise and describe the physical and human features of places and begin to do this within a wider locational framework. They describe how physical and human processes can change the features of places and how these changes affect the lives and activities of people living there.

> Level 5: Pupils show increasing depth of knowledge and understanding of aspects of the geography of the UK and the wider world. They use this to describe physical and human characteristics of places within a wider locational and contextual framework. They describe and begin to explain geographical patterns.[1]

I recall creating level descriptors based on these generic statements for each of the assessments pupils completed. These descriptors were aligned to the concept or process that we were assessing. As I'm sure is the case for many teachers at this time in education, we ended up with hundreds of descriptors for all assessments across our Key Stage 3 curriculum. I went back into the archives of my USB to find one of these assessments to illustrate just what I was using to assess progress. For Year 8 one of these assessments were based on pupils investigating and making judgements on the conditions of employment for fashion workers, producing a newspaper report with the aim to reach the illusive Level 7 descriptor. This led to many bespoke descriptors that were specifically written for this assessment to judge pupil's performance.

The majority of pupils were not awarded a Level 7, not just because they didn't have enough understanding of the knowledge required to apply to the task set, but also, in all honesty, I wasn't confident that I really knew myself what the performance looked like for these different levels. This was because there was a very fine difference between one level to the other, it was difficult to decide

---

1. QCA. (2010) 'The National Curriculum: Level descriptions for subjects'. Retrieved from: www. bit.ly/3aIF89p

---

Year 8: FASHION VICTIMS

ADMC – A: To investigate the conditions of employment for fashion workers.
B: To decide if fashion workers are victims of 'westernised' fashion.

Level 3: Describe briefly the condition of sweatshops. Make a brief decision on whether it is fair or not. You have produced a presentation that identifies a number of features found in factory sweatshops.

Level 4: Describe in some detail the condition of sweatshops in the production of westernised clothing. You have made a more detailed decision on whether the conditions of employment are fair, with a supporting reason on whether you think the workers are victims of fashion. Your presentation contains a range of material to illustrate factory conditions. There is evidence of independent research.

Level 5: Describe and explain in detail the conditions of factory sweatshops with supporting explanations of why these conditions exist. You have justified your decision on whether workers are victims of fashion. When justifying your reason you should give a detailed explanation of how you arrived at your decision. Remember to use words like 'because'.

Level 6: You have provided a balanced answer on the conditions of employment experiences by factory sweatshop employees. You have considered the views of all those involved in the process. Included in your presentation will be an analysis of the views of the different people involved, as well as your own.

Level 7: You appreciate the changes that may occur in the conditions of employment come from a range of global influences. What would happen if the western world stopped buying fashionable clothing?

---

which piece of work to award a Level 4 or Level 5, with the determining factor seemingly on whether the student had begun to offer some explanation. I recall, while marking pupil's work, contemplating whether the pupil had demonstrated enough supporting explanations to be awarded a Level 5? If I was debating this when marking my own pupil work, it also became a lengthy conversation at department meetings when we were moderating. What one teacher though was evidence of enough explanation was different to someone else.

Additionally, a further determining factor when considering whether the pupil had done enough to be awarded a level was the variety and complexity of subject-specific vocabulary that the pupil had used. As a department we would use this as an indication of whether the pupil had achieved a level, but this didn't demonstrate understanding of the knowledge. This led to what I referred to earlier, teachers like myself applying a 'best fit' approach with pupils allocated a level if it was felt they had achieved what was necessary for that level. The degree of subjectivity was high and inevitably it raised questions to me on the reliability of the levels we were awarding to the pieces of work being assessed.

Alongside this, even more troubling for me as I reflect on how I assessed; I was suggesting that for this isolated piece of work, based on one aspect of the curriculum, the pupil had demonstrated enough evidence to achieve a specific level. This was never meant to be the purpose of the national curriculum levels. They were designed to suggest how a pupil had performed at the end of Key Stage 2 or 3 following coverage of the full programmes of study. The distorted use of levels for teacher assessments was one of the rationales for their removal, something that was highlighted in the governments commissioned report on life after levels in September 2015.

'Too often levels became viewed as thresholds and teaching became focused on getting pupils across the next threshold instead of ensuring they were secure in the knowledge and understanding defined in the programmes of study. Depth and breadth of understanding were sometimes sacrificed in favour of pace. Levels also used a "bit fit" model, which meant that a pupil could have serious gaps in their knowledge and understanding, but still be placed within the level. This meant it wasn't always clear exactly which areas of the curriculum the child was secure in and where the gaps were.'[2]

The setting and marking of these assessments were the first steps in the process of assessing. After completing the assessment, I would record the levels achieved by pupils in my mark book and then the focus was on analysing the levels that pupils had attained across the teaching group. During this period, there was a lot of pressure on teachers to ensure pupils achieved their expected target level at the end of the year, with flight paths indicating every child's expected progress over the course of Key Stage 3 dependent on their starting points from Key Stage 2. Thinking back there was a definite shift in focus, with a greater emphasis on moving pupils through the levels, thus shifting the weight from assessing the acquisition of knowledge at the end of the programme of study, to the rate of progress. Therefore, pushing pupils through the level thresholds regardless of whether their understanding was secure within that level. I remember senior leaders often frowned upon suggesting that several pupils were not on target to achieve their expected level at the end of the academic year. It also became an expectation, the norm, that most pupils would achieve and exceed the national expectation.

I recall when some pupils switched teaching groups that I would often disagree with the level that the previous teacher suggested the pupil was currently working at or could achieve by the end of the year. This was the problem with how the levels were being interpreted by different teachers. I remember conversations happening in the staffroom after the first few weeks

2. Department of Education. (2015) 'Final report of the Commission on Assessment without Levels'. London: The Stationery Office. Retrieved from: www.bit.ly/3cCS6at

of the new Year 7 pupils arriving, discussing how colleagues didn't agree with the level pupils had been awarded at the end of their primary education. How can that pupil possibly have achieved a Level 5? The work I've seen so far from them demonstrates they are working far below that level. Then add into the mix the fact that inevitably the curriculum diet pupils received outside of the core subjects was increasingly variable between feeder schools. The starting point for Year 7 pupils who were studying subjects like geography, history and languages was below their anticipated starting point by these flight paths. This created difficulties and resentment amongst secondary school teachers who had to miraculously get pupils to move along their anticipated flight path. When considering all these factors, it is not surprising that assessment became focused on pushing through thresholds rather than reflecting on pupils' acquisition of knowledge.

When it came to provide a report to parents about their child's attainment, there seemed to be a greater focus on what level we felt their child was currently working at, such as a Level 4. Also, alongside this, whether their child was on track to achieve their expected level at the end of the academic year. There was a focus on labelling the pupil rather than unpicking with parents the knowledge they were secure in and the knowledge that needed greater practice. It was not that important what level they were working at, the focus should have been on where their knowledge gaps were. When I think back to my dialogue with parents it usually involved the following comments:

'Tom's target level for the end the year is...'

'In Tom's recent assessments he has achieved the following level...'

'In order for Tom to achieve his target level for the end of the year he needs to demonstrate the following in his upcoming assessments...'

When it was time to provide feedback to pupils, we created a gimmicky process involving a set of levelled towers where we would allocate pupils to a tower based on what level we felt they were working at following their performance on each individual formal assessment. For example, if a pupil achieved a Level 5, we would say they had climbed to the top of the Petronas Tower. We set the expectation to pupils that if they were climbing up the different level of towers, they were becoming better geographers! This inevitably resulted in a distraction away from pupil's awareness of their strengths and areas for improvement in relation to the core concepts and processes in geography. The language amongst pupils was, 'I want to get to the Freedom Tower', which led to a disconnect between their understanding of where their gaps in knowledge were and, instead, the aspiration to achieve the higher tower status.

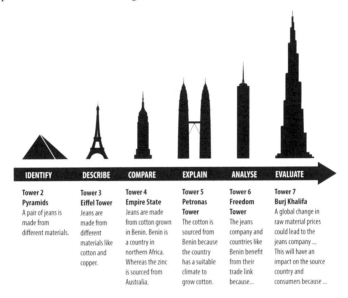

IDENTIFY	DESCRIBE	COMPARE	EXPLAIN	ANALYSE	EVALUATE
Tower 2 Pyramids A pair of jeans is made from different materials.	Tower 3 Eiffel Tower Jeans are made from different materials like cotton and copper.	Tower 4 Empire State Jeans are made from cotton grown in Benin. Benin is a country in northern Africa. Whereas the zinc is sourced from Australia.	Tower 5 Petronas The cotton is sourced from Benin because the country has a suitable climate to grow cotton.	Tower 6 Freedom Tower The jeans company and countries like Benin benefit from their trade link because...	Tower 7 Burj Khalifa A global change in raw material prices could lead to the jeans company ... This will have an impact on the source country and consumers because ...

There are still aspects of how we assess pupils that for me still seem disconnected to the purpose. At GCSE level, many teachers are still expected to track whether a pupil is 'on target' to achieve their expected grade at the end of their GCSE course. The targets set are based on pupil's end of Key Stage 2 performance, which is then used to provide an indication of what grade they are expected to achieve at the end of Year 11. From this prediction, teachers are asked to advice school leaders if pupils are 'on track' to achieve their expected grade at the end of the course and their working at target when whole-school data drops are requested. The problem with this is we cannot accurately say if a pupil is 'on track' to achieve their GCSE target. Firstly, when teachers make a judgement about pupils work there is the inevitability of subconscious bias, as explained by the economist Daniel Kahneman. He identifies a particular form of bias, the anchoring effect, which he believes occurs when we try to think of a value for an unknown quantity before estimating that quantity.[3] When teachers assess a piece of work for a child that we have taught for a length of time, we

3.   Education Endowment Foundation. (No date) 'Assessing and Monitoring Pupil Progress', Education Endowment Foundation [Online]. Retrieved from: www.bit.ly/339aSBR

introduce bias into the process. This leads to marks being raised for pupils we may feel could have performed better, pupils that we may get on well with or, on the flip side, award lower marks for SEN pupils or those who regularly display difficult behaviour in lessons.

When pupils complete an in-school summative assessment, like an end of topic test, end of year exam or a mock exam, this will usually be based on one paper or several components of the subject. The problem with suggesting that a pupil is on or off 'track' from these summative assessments is:

1. Pupils will be preparing for one aspect of their GCSE rather than the whole course.
2. Pupils may already know what parts of the subject is being assessed in the school assessment.
3. Teachers are using historical grade boundaries, which are set based on the performance of a cohort in each examination series.
4. Teachers may not have the expertise when applying mark schemes and, therefore, suggested grade outcomes from these summative assessments will likely be inaccurate.
5. The assessment could be completed in a classroom environment that won't represent the same conditions that pupils will be exposed to for their actual examinations.
6. Teachers may set up assessments that provide students with too much or too little time to complete, which is not representative of the real examination.

Therefore, it is difficult for teachers to know if a pupil is going to achieve a specific grade or if they are in fact working at a specific grade at different checkpoints along their GCSE journey.

This distorted understanding of how to assess pupils over time has created significant challenges for teachers in the primary and secondary phases. Inevitably, the word assessment has been associated with negative connotations due to inevitability of greater workload because of the increased frequency and depth of marking, the associated feedback, the crunching of data, the necessity to use these in-school tests to ascertain progress, and increased pressures to use these assessments for accountability. As a profession we seem to have for many years lost the real purpose of assessment in schools.

Whilst the removal of levels has been a step in the right direction, the reporting of GCSE grades still demonstrates that teachers are being asked to provide superficial data that quite simply isn't accurate. In some cases, the removal of levels has been replaced with the use of grades from Year 7. Trying to suggest what grade a student is working at in relation to a GCSE grade is quite simply nonsense. Consequently, there needs be a culture shift to modify how assessment is being used in schools for it to be a decisive pedagogy tool that supports the facilitation of learning, not a term that is used for accountability or to driving school improvement. This is reinforced by the Evidence Based Education and SchoolsWeek review on 'what every teacher needs to know about assessment':

'Teachers need to reclaim assessment and put it to work as the servant of the curriculum and of pedagogy so that assessment works for learning.'[4]

There are many other definitions of assessment that have been shared in the education sphere, and what all definitions seem to have in common is a similar rationale as to why we assess pupils and its powerful influence. For teachers to understand what pupils know and what they need to do to close their knowledge gap, demonstrated by the World Bank's definition:

'Assessment of student learning is a powerful agent for change in schools by informing policymakers about the learning outcomes of the nation's students, helping teachers understand how to improve classroom instruction, and influencing societies as they think about education quality and learning goals.'[5]

So, now that we have reviewed what I believe are the past and present issues associated with assessment practices in schools to assess pupils as well as those echoed in wider assessment reviews, I believe as a profession we need to take a step back and consider the basic principles of using assessment in the classroom.

Scriven (1967) suggested some of the earliest work on the distinction between summative and formative roles in programme evaluation where he identified summative as 'information to judge the overall value of an educational programme', whereas formative evaluation was believed to be used to provide focus on 'facilitating programme improvement'. This was further emphasised by Bloom (1969) who used similar definitions of the terms but in the context of pupils instead of the evaluations of programmes. Bloom was

4.   Evidence Based Education (2018) 'What #EveryTeacher needs to know about assessment: a panel event', *Evidence Based Education* [Online] 27 November. Retrieved from: www.bit. ly/2ItEOPJ
5.   ResourcEd: a promethean blog (no date) 'Student assessment: A complete look at the state of assessment in education', ResourcEd: a promethean blog [Online]. Retrieved from: www.bit. ly/392XIaX

one of the first to explore the differences between the use of formative and summative assessment with pupils. In his research, Bloom emphasised that the main reason for the use of formative evaluation was to 'provide feedback and correctives at each stage of the teaching-learning process' whereas summative assessment was 'employed to judge what the learner had achieved at the end of a course or programme'. He continued to develop his research on the benefits of formative assessment during the early 1970s, identifying that teachers could utilise formative assessment to divide a class into 'cooperative groups' that would be based on the necessary requirements to correct the knowledge gaps required for pupils to learn. This would then provide the conditions for teachers to use targeted teaching strategies.

During the late 1990s, Paul Black and Dylan Wiliam built on the previous research from Scriven and Bloom, as well as other researchers, which led to the start of what we know as 'Assessment for Learning' (AfL). Black and William published the findings from their research in the book widely known as *Inside the Black Box*. In their review they concluded that 'there is no other way of raising standards for which such a strong *prima facie* case can be made'. The evidence from their review indicated that the use of formative assessment was one of the single most effective strategies to support pupils in achieving learning intentions across all education phases. In their research they indicated that when teachers used formative assessment this led to an effect size of between .4 and .7.

This led to a wave of AfL strategies in schools to embed assessment practices, including the concept of having an AfL toolkit to choose strategies to use in your classroom. However, after further research and reflection on the evolving use of AfL strategies in classrooms, Wiliam believes he should have used the term 'responsive teaching'. This is something Harry Fletcher-Wood highlights and explores expertly in his fantastic book *Responsive Teaching*:

'When assessment is formative, the aim is to reveal pupils' weaknesses so that the teacher can act on them. When assessment is summative, the aim is to give pupils a final grade, and so there can be pressure to try to conceal and gloss over misunderstandings. Indeed, formative assessment is so different from summative assessment that Wiliam has said that he wished he had called AfL, "responsive teaching", rather than using the word assessment.'

This view of formative assessment as responsive teaching is a useful term to establish strategies to apply in the classroom. It provides a clear indication that when teachers are being responsive, they could be providing 'in the moment' necessary adjustments to teaching that reflects the data we collect after checking for understanding following knowledge input. This was summarised by

Ramaprasad's who outlined three aspects that are required for consideration when assessing learning, establishing where pupils are in their learning, where pupils are going, and what needs to be done to get them to the point of where they need to be.

In review of this research and to establish a clear framework for the use of formative assessment in the learning process, Wiliam and Thompson provided five overarching strategies to conceptualise the process:

1. Clarifying and sharing learning intentions and criteria for success.
2. Engineering effective classroom discussions and other learning tasks that elicit evidence of student understanding.
3. Providing feedback that moves learners forward.
4. Activating students as instructional resources for one another.
5. Activating students as the owners of their own learning.[6]

The interaction of these overarching strategies and their links to Ramaprasad's three aspects are shown in the table.[7]

	Where the learner is going	Where the learner is right now	How to get there
Teacher	1. Clarify learning intentions and criteria for success	2. Engineering effective classroom discussions and other learning tasks that elicit evidence of student understanding	3. Providing feedback that moves learners forward
Peer	Understanding and sharing learning intentions and criteria for success	4. Activating students as instructional resources for one another	
Learner	Understanding learning intentions and criteria for success	5. Activating students as the owners of their own learning	

In 2004, William, Lee, Harrison and Black conducted additional research in the influence of formative assessment, examining the achievement of secondary pupils in maths and science who were either exposed to formative assessment compared with those that were not. The outcomes of the research indicated a

6. Wiliam, D. and Thompson, M. (2007) 'Integrating assessment with instruction: what will it take to make it work?', in C. A. Dwyer (ed.) *The future of assessment: shaping teaching and learning* (pp. 53-82). Mahwah, NJ: Lawrence Erlbaum Associates.
7. Black, P. and Wiliam, D. (2009) 'Developing the Theory of Formative Assessment', *Educational Assessment, Evaluation and Accountability* 21 (1) p. 8.

mean effect size of 0.32, further strengthening that when teachers are trained to implement formative assessment strategies it will have a positive effect on pupil outcomes.

Determining learning – can we?

Professor Robert Coe outlined in his inaugural lecture at Durham University's School of Education that determining whether pupils are learning is difficult to establish because learning is happening in the mind. He articulated that when we are teaching or someone is observing a lesson, they are inevitably watching pupils perform, therefore we can make assumptions about whether learning is taking place. This has in the past led to what he coined as poor proxies for learning. Professor Robert Coe outlined in his augural lecture at Durham University's School of Education that determining whether pupils are learning is difficult to establish because learning is happening in the mind. He articulated that:

1. Students are busy: lots of work is done (especially written work).
2. Students are engaged, interested and motivated.
3. Students are getting attention, feedback and explanations.
4. Classroom is ordered, calm and under control.
5. Curriculum has been 'covered' (*i.e.* presented to students in some form).
6. (At least some) students have supplied correct answers (whether or not they really understood them or could reproduce them independently).[8]

David Didau provided some suggestions for what we might consider as good proxies for learning:

1. Concentrate on relevant examples and non-examples.
2. Retrieve what they have been taught in previous lessons.
3. Apply concepts to new examples.
4. Engage in practice drills (which may involve repetition of formulas and procedures).
5. Answers questions without cues or prompts.[9]

If we are to assess the learning that has taken place, we should be clear about the difference between learning and performance. As I discussed in Chapter 2,

8. Centre for Evaluation & Monitoring. (2015) 'What makes great teaching?', *IB World Regional Conference* [Online] 31 October. Retrieved from: www.bit.ly/2wIUTOX
9. Didau, D. (2016) 'More good proxies for learning', *Learning Spy* [Online] 28 November. Retrieved from: www.bit.ly/39IxuLU

we know that the evidence suggests for learning to take place there needs to be a change in long-term memory. This requires pupils to engage in a 'healthy struggle' and practice transferring knowledge into new scenarios. If we are to potentially assess whether our pupils are learning, we should look to create assessment opportunities that cumulatively build on knowledge to new scenarios over time. This is what we will now explore in assessment design.

Designing assessment

If we want to make the most of assessing pupil's learning, we must invest time and support for teachers in the designing of effective and efficient assessments. In many cases, assessment structures in schools are often designed to encapsulate pupils learning of concepts and processes at the end of a topic, usually titled an end of unit assessment. This structure continues throughout the duration of the academic year with assessments determining progress for the isolated topics of study outlined in the programmes of study or specifications. These assessments are often designed to replicate what pupils would expect to see in the 'real' examination. The problem with this assessment structure is just because pupils may perform well in one end of unit assessment it doesn't mean they learnt the concepts and processes when faced with applying the same knowledge in new contexts at the end of their course. This is because they may not have retained what they have learnt.

In contrast, designing assessments so that they are cumulative to enable pupils to practice concepts and processes from topics over time. Instead of testing pupil's understanding of the most recent topic of study, use cumulative assessments to include knowledge from previous topics to allow pupils to continually practice bringing knowledge back to mind to strengthen schemas. Take an example below of Year 9 history pupils learning about Weimar government, the structure of cumulative assessment may look like the following.

		Solutions from Stresesmann
	Revolts against Weimar	Revolts against Weimar
	Problems of 1923	Problems of 1923
Legacy of WWI	Legacy of WWI	Legacy of WWI
Weimar Constitution	Weimar Constitution	Weimar Constitution
Opposition to Weimar	Opposition to Weimar	Opposition to Weimar

TIME →

In this history example, the structure of the assessments allows for the building blocks of knowledge to be increased over time. This strategy provides the opportunity for pupils to recall aspects of concepts and processes that will be important to bring back to the forefront of their memory to enable them to apply knowledge to another context.

Hinge questions

Hinge questions are a possible strategy to formatively assess pupil's acquisition of knowledge at a suitable point in a learning sequence, referred to as the 'hinge point'. It would be counterintuitive for me to suggest when this hinge point would be in a learning sequence because this will inevitably differ from one subject to another and within a subject's core concepts or processes that pupils are studying. It is, therefore, important that teachers have the autonomy to use hinge questions at the points that they feel is appropriate. Additionally, for hinge questions to be an effective assessment tools this will require formulating a multiple-choice question that has been carefully constructed so that it has several options that are wrong but could plausibly be the right answer. Alongside, the 'wrong' answers, formulating these options is equally important. This is because if they have been carefully designed it should also allow you as the teacher to reveal misconceptions and assumptions that pupils may have. Consequently, creating the best hinge question requires collaborative modelling and practice with other teachers.

For example, when a science teacher has been teaching about rates of reaction an example of a hinge question that the teacher could ask their class:

HOW DOES A CATALYST INCREASE THE RATE OF A REACTION?

a. It speeds up the rate of reaction without being used up.
b. It provides an alternative pathway for the reaction to happen at a lower activation energy.
c. It provides an alternative pathway which speeds up the rate of reaction.
d. It doesn't get used up so increases the rate of reaction and can then be extracted at the end.

When a geography teacher is teaching global biomes to pupils and developing an understanding of why variations in air temperatures exist might ask the following hinge question:

WHAT IS THE MAIN REASON WHY AIR TEMPERATURE VARIES ACROSS THE GLOBE?

    a. The Earth orbits the sun.
    b. The Earth orbits the sun at an angle.
    c. The Earth is a sphere.
    d. The Earth has a hot core.

The creation of an effective multiple-choice question and when to introduce the hinge point in the learning sequence is the first few steps. After this, it is important to consider how pupils will provide their choice to the teacher.

In order to truly get an accurate assessment of what pupils have learnt it is important that answers to the hinge questions are delivered simultaneously. Therefore, asking pupils to put their hands up to provide their response may not be the most appropriate in assessing understanding. It is likely from research around human behaviour that pupils will inevitably end up 'following the crowd' by delaying their response by a few seconds to gauge the thoughts of their peers. This will provide a false response for teachers to know who 'gets it' and who needs further guidance and support. A possible alternative is the use of coloured cards to represent the A-D options, or creating online quizzes using websites such as Survey Monkey, Plicker or Class Marker. The use of online quizzing through Google Forms and its effectiveness in the classroom is unpicked by Dawn Cox discussing this as part of a formative assessment strategy in her spotlight at the end of this chapter. Once you have checked for understanding through the pupil's responses you can then decide on whether there is a need to re-teach to dispel any misconceptions or move on in the learning sequence. A possible thought is to put in a threshold based on how many pupils should be expected to get the question write to move on. For example, you may decide that, in order to move on, 70% of pupils need to get the right answer. This will be dependent on how important the concept or process is linked to the next stage of learning. However, if we can design effective hinge questions and use them at appropriate points in the learning sequence this can help to reduce the need for re-teaching concepts or processes that pupils fail to grasp after assessment.

Sharing learning intentions

Learning intentions, or what can be commonly referred to as learning objectives, goals, or targets are a common feature of today's classrooms. When we share the learning intentions this creates the conditions to spark the active involvement of students in their own learning and provide the right conditions for students to be able to assess themselves against the knowledge and skills for each subject, as well as creating an awareness of what's required to improve. This allows them to focus their attention on what is expected and use deliberate practice to work towards making knowledge more permanent. If pupils don't know the learning path they are taking, they will not understand the knowledge that is required for them to be successful.

However, the sharing of learning intentions under the guise of 'learning objectives' and 'learning outcomes' has in some respect become merely white noise to pupils, something that is done at the start of lesson by teachers because it is a requirement from a lesson pro forma or checklist. This concern was echoed by David Didau, 'the use of learning objectives has, all too often, become a reflective box ticking exercise with little or no thought behind it'. In this approach, it can lead to teachers putting up learning objectives at the beginning of a lesson to 'comply' to school requirements, which lead to them becoming wallpaper for pupils, where they write them down and move on. I'm not saying this means that the sharing of learning intentions should be abandoned, but rather the way in which they are implemented and used in lesson should be reviewed.

When teachers share the learning intentions and provide clear links to the wider related concepts and processes this contributes towards supporting the development of pupil's metacognitive knowledge and self-regulation. Therefore, it's important that these learning intentions are focused on what they will be learning rather than what they will be doing. In Chapter 2, I discussed the idea of sharing the learning journey and knowledge checklists with pupils for them to develop into more reflective and self-regulated learners. For pupils to engage and improve their own learning, become self-regulated, they need to know the core knowledge that they are learning. Consequently, when introducing new concepts or processes along the learning journey it's important we spend time to connect these intentions to the wider knowledge of our subjects for pupils to move forward in their learning. When we provide pupils with guided and explicit instructions this is more likely to see improve pupil outcomes.

In Kirschner, Sweller and Clark's research they stated that 'controlled experiments almost uniformly indicate that when dealing with novel information, learners should be explicitly shown what to do and how to do it'.[10] It is particularly important for lower ability pupils who benefit from knowing where the lesson is going and its connections to the wider concepts and processes within our subjects. The anxiety associated with learning is often high for many of the pupils we teach and knowing where the lesson is heading, and for what reason, can help to reduce these anxiety levels, providing improved conditions for effective learning.

10. Kirschner, P., Sweller, J. and Clark, R. (2006) 'Why Minimal Guidance During Instruction Does Not Work: An Analysis of the Failure of Constructivist Discovery, Problem-Based, Experiential, and Inquiry-Based Teaching', *Educational Psychologist* 41 (2) p. 79.

Exit tickets

The use of exit tickets is a possible strategy for teachers to capture and assess pupil's understanding of knowledge and provides an opportunity for pupils to reflect and strengthen memory. There have been many reservations about the use of exit tickets however, if used as a strategy in combination with retrieval practice which I discussed in Chapter 2, it can be a powerful tool to assess pupil's learning. Researcher Robert, J. Marzano explored the use of exit tickets in the art and science classrooms. From this research, he identified there are four prompts that can be understood using exit tickets:

1. **Prompt 1** – Generating information about pupil's level of understanding. For example, how would you rate your current level of understanding of what we did today?
2. **Prompt 2** – Generating opportunities to encourage self-assessment. For example, how hard did you work today?
3. **Prompt 3** – Gaining an understanding about the instructional strategies used during the class period. For example, how did you find the delivery of the knowledge?
4. **Prompt 4** – An opportunity for the pupil to communicate with the teacher. For example, how can I support you in understanding the content?[11]

Questioning

One of the key characteristics of our classrooms is discussions between teacher to pupil, pupil to teacher, and pupil to pupil, with the day consisting of asking hundreds of questions to elicit an understanding of what pupil's know. In one research study, Morgan and Saxton exclaimed, 'it is better to have a classroom full of unanswered questions than unanswered answers'.[12]

In another study, it was found that teachers ask questions for a variety of reasons:

- When teachers ask questions, this helps to keep pupils actively involved in lessons.
- The act of answering questions allows pupils to openly express their ideas and thoughts.

---

11. Marzano, R. J. (2012) 'Art and science of teaching: The many uses of exit tickets', *Educational Leadership* 70 (2) pp. 80-81.
12. Morgan, N. and Saxton, J. (1991) *Teaching Questioning and Learning.* New York, NY: Routledge.

- The act of questioning pupils provides an opportunity for other pupils to listen to different explanations from their peers.
- The process of asking questions can support teachers in pacing their lessons.
- The use of questions helps teachers to evaluate pupil learning and revise their lessons.[13]

In Rosenshine's paper 'Principle of Instructions', one of the ten principles that expert teachers do is ask many questions and check the responses received from all pupils. By asking many questions during a lesson it can provide the opportunity for pupils to practice verbalising new information and create connections to prior learning. Rosenshine indicates from his research that when teachers ask lots of questions it allows them 'to determine how well the material has been learnt'.[14] This will support teachers in determining the next stage of the learning process.

There are usually two key differences between the types of questions that teachers ask in the classroom. The first is defined as low-level cognitive questions that focus on knowledge recall, such as 'Who are the main characters in *An Inspector Calls*?', 'What is hydraulic action?' or 'What year did World War I begin?'

High-level cognitive questions are the second type, which require pupils to think more deeply. These types of questions require pupils to not only recall knowledge but also apply it explain, analyse or evaluate.

Wilen and Clegg conducted research on questioning techniques and suggested that teachers could adopt the following to support pupils' learning:

- Phrase the question clearly.
- Ask questions of primarily an academic nature.
- Allow three or five seconds of wait time after asking a question before requesting a student's response, particularly when high-cognitive level questions are asked.
- Encourage students to respond in some way to each question asked.
- Elicit a high percentage of correct responses from students and assist with incorrect responses.
- Probe students' responses to have them clarify ideas, support a point of view, or extend their thinking.

13. Brualdi Timmins, A. C. (1998) 'Classroom Questions', *Practical Assessment, Research, and Evaluations,* 6 (article no. 6).
14. Rosenshine, B. (2012) 'Principles of Instruction', *American Educator* [Online] Spring. Retrieved from: www.bit.ly/2vX3cGy

- Acknowledge correct responses from students and use praise specifically and discriminately.[15]

Whilst asking lots of questions is more effective in formatively assessing pupils understanding, the level of success will be dependent on the type of questions asked.

There are several strategies teachers can use to develop a two-way dialogue to encourage pupils to verbalise their learning, of which some of these have been given an identification by the excellent work of Doug Lemov in *Teach Like a Champion*:

- **Cold call** – this means all pupils are aware that they may be chosen to offer an answer, rather than the dominant voices becoming the norm in your classroom. For example, *what are the four processes of erosion, Tom?*
- **Wait time** – when posing a question to a pupil, allow a few seconds for pupils to process what you have asked before offering a response.
- **Stretch it** – when pupils get the right answer to a question, add a layer of complexity by asking them a harder question to challenge pupils thinking. For example, after asking an initial question, follow it up with a 'why' or 'how'.
- **Format matters** – support pupils in responding to questions in a format that communicates their ideas to reflect excellence within your subject.[16]

In the following three spotlights Dawn, Aidan and Ben talk about how they have used assessment in their classrooms.

Teacher Spotlight
Dawn Cox,
a religious education teacher

Teacher bio-sketch: Dawn is a teacher and head of RE, currently working in north Essex. She has held a wide variety of roles in schools in her teaching career including Head of RE, AST, SLE and SLT member. She is a chartered teacher who is interested in curriculum, assessment and pedagogy. Dawn writes on her blog missdcoxblog.wordpress.com and has several current RE publications. You can find her tweeting at @missdcox

15. Brualdi Timmins, A. C. (1998) 'Classroom Questions', *Practical Assessment, Research, and Evaluations*, 6 (article no. 6).
16. Lemov, D. (2014) *Teach Like a Champion 2.0*. San Francisco, CA: Jossey-Bass.

As RE teachers we have many classes and one of the things that I am always mindful of is our mark load. At Key Stage 3 we use two formal, department wide, forms of assessment alongside informal assessment from questioning etc. One of these is fully summative and the other is used formatively and summatively.

Firstly, we use online, multiple choice quizzes using Google Forms. Students take the quizzes at the start, middle and end of each topic. Each quiz has approximately 30 questions that cover the content of the topic being taught. They have three or four options and always have an 'I don't know yet' option.

What do Sunni Muslims believe that is different to Shi'a Muslims? *

◯ Ali was the first leader after Muhammad's death

◯ I don't know yet

◯ There was no leader after Muhammad

◉ The leader after Muhammad was Abu Bakr

The majority of Muslims in the world are.... *

◯ Atheists

◯ Christian

◯ Shi'a

◯ I don't know yet

◉ Sunni

We have recently changed it so there is only one correct answer for each question. Previously we found that having multiple correct option answers was confusing and ended up not being representative of what they knew. Students are strongly discouraged from guessing. We can generally tell if they ignore this advice in their answer result sheet as there are lots of incorrect answers, in which case we may get them to repeat the quiz.

Students are not given their score; we don't want them trying to be competitive with others or with themselves, we want to know what they do/don't know.

We look at the series of scores over the year to see if their score has increased. When it comes to year exams, we get students to complete the quizzes from each topic completed so far in that year and are just compiling one separate quiz that asks questions from the previous year to promote retrieval from all prior topics.

The benefits of the quizzes are that they don't require any teacher marking, they are objectives so this makes the assessment more reliable and, with caveats, can be used to inform our reports on student progress.

The possible drawbacks of the quizzes are students guessing the answers, having the time to create the quizzes in the first place and the requirement to access IT to complete the quizzes (we use iPads).

This is the only fully summative assessment we do; students don't get feedback and we don't use it to inform future learning. Everything else has feedback and students improve their work.

Alongside the quizzes we also get students to complete one piece of assessed work per half term. This is a written piece that draws on the things learnt throughout the topic. We have identified the key 'skills' that we want our students to develop over Key Stage 3 and each assessment focuses on some of these. For example, using religious texts in their answers and considering a variety of arguments on a topic. Over Key Stage 3 we develop these skills so that by the end, the students should be using them fluently.

We are currently adapting the tasks so that they are posed as enquiry questions that allow students to use what they've learnt to develop a comprehensive answer.

To ensure that our workload is manageable we have designed a criteria-based marking system with a simple tick sheet. These criteria are shared with students and developed over the key stage. They are recorded on a tracker for an easy to view summary. This is summative in that we look at the overview of assessments for reporting but it is also formative as students get to learn from how they do and get to repeat using the specific skill.

		Year 7						Year 8					
	Term	1a	1b	2a	2b	3a	3b	1a	1b	2a	2b	3a	3b
Reasons	For												
	Against												
Developing reasons	Example/Evidence												
	Quotes												
Knowledge	Key beliefs & teachings												
	Keywords												
	Textual sources												
Evaluation	Justified conclusion												

For each of these assessments, students are given feedback on what they need to do to improve their work We then give them time to act on the feedback, with 'green pen' work. This can be based on developing the knowledge included and/or developing the 'skill' that the assessment focuses on.

The benefits of this system are that:

- it focuses on key skills we want them to develop, which feeds into GCSE without being GCSE questions or mark schemes.
- it makes things as simple as possible for teachers that have many groups' work to mark.
- we can see an overview of what they have/n't shown in this piece of work.

One of the biggest issues with assessing written work is subjectivity, which undermines its reliability and the validity of how we use the assessment. We have tried to minimise this as much as possible, however I am acutely aware that our system falls foul of this, as with many written subjects. We've tried to counter this as much as possible by having clear criteria, however it is still problematical.

It is also questionable to suggest that one piece of written work is representative of their learning. There is a tendency to see fluent written work in a positive light when it may not include depth of subject knowledge. We sometimes provide students with writing frames to support the structure of their writing so that their knowledge and understanding can come through even if their style of writing isn't articulate.

Teacher Spotlight
Aidan Severs,
primary deputy headteacher

Teacher bio-sketch: Aidan Severs is a primary deputy head in an all-through school in Bradford. He writes about education at his blog thatboycanteach.co.uk as well as for other outlets such as the TES. Aidan still loves to teach. You can find him tweeting at @thatboycanteach

There is no teaching without assessment.

But there can be assessment without teaching. There can, and should be, assessment before teaching, to be precise. As a class teacher in primary you don't have to have taught your class anything about fractions before you assess their current understanding of them (unless you're a Year 1 teacher and are introducing the concept for the first time). In fact, before you teach them your year group's fraction content it is very important that you find out what they know already. In this instance you would do some pre-assessment to inform your planning and teaching – this is formative assessment.

In an English unit focusing on writing adverbial phrases, for example, you wouldn't wait until you had finished teaching before you assessed how the children were getting along with it. You would sit down with your children's books and work out how successful each child has been after each lesson. Additionally, if you had structured your lesson time well enough, you would have already seen within the lesson how well each child was doing. If you then use the information you have gained from that exercise to inform future learning, this is also formative assessment.

Formative assessment is your friend and you should do it all day, every day.

Summative assessment is a little different and is often seen as the enemy – the thing that we teachers are judged by, those results that get sent to governors, parents, league tables and the like. They are the product of either testing or a teacher's judgement based on a set of predetermined criteria. Summative assessment sums up what a child has learnt over a given period of time, whether during a unit of work, a half term, a term, a year, or a key stage. It is potentially useful for tracking children's progress and attainment over time.

So, in short, formative assessment is what you should be doing all the time in order to inform your teaching and summative assessment should be completed at an end point in order to sum up what a child understands or can do at a particular moment in time.

It's clear as to which kind of assessment is most useful for teachers in the classroom: formative assessment, hands down.

Formative assessment doesn't have to be complicated. In fact, the simpler the better, and for your wellbeing's sake, the quicker the better too. Here's just one way of completing formative assessment so that it feeds forward into your next day's teaching, ensuring that all children are working on exactly what they need to be working on:

Let's go back to that sequence of maths teaching that we referred to earlier. You've done some fractions work – let's say it's some work on equivalent fractions – and at the end of the session you want to get an overall picture of where the class are at, as well as a good idea of which individuals have struggled and which ones really need a little more challenge.

Now, hopefully you will have seen a good deal of the children's work during the lesson, and will have already provided some children with some additional help – a minute, on-the-spot cycle of assessment informing teaching. However, to be realistic, no one can see all the work in all the books within the lesson time.

So you sit down with your books and spend 15 minutes reviewing them, finishing off the last bits of simple marking (indicating right or wrong in the case of maths) and getting the sense of how well the class has done. At this point it is a good idea to start grouping children based on the success of the lesson just gone. You could make physical piles of books: one for those who really got it and need further challenge, one for those who just need a little more practice, one for those who need some re-teaching due to a particular shared misconception (*e.g.* they all believe that ¼ is equal to 4/10), one for those who have more individual specific needs and who might benefit from a bit of 1:1 time. You get the idea. Instead of making tottering piles of books you might simply choose to use a page in your notebook to make lists of who needs what in the next lesson – no pre-made format necessary.

Now you have some ready-made 'groups' for the next session in the sequence, but what are they going to do in that time? This is where your assessment can influence much more than just the tasks you set. It can also inform how you structure your lesson.

Continuing with our example, that group of children who need re-teaching don't need to be joined by those who need a further challenge. Nor do the children who just need more practice of the same need to sit through repeat explanations and modelling. Gather the children who need re-teaching around you – some dynamic, ever-changing seating planning is necessary here – and let the rest of the children get on with it.

Of course, those children who needed moving on will need a self-directed, accessible activity to be working on whilst you teach the smaller group. You could provide simple step-by-step worked examples if it is something that they can't just immediately apply previous learning to. They also might need some way of self-checking their progress, so have some answers printed out ready to minimise disruption whilst you teach.

Now, once you've finished the re-teaching and that group are hard at work practising what you've just shown them, you can get out and about in the lesson to carry out that all-important, on-the-spot formative assessment, checking in on those who are most likely to need help or encouragement as a priority.

Some of those who were practicing the previous lesson's learning might now be ready to move on to the more challenging work. Once you have identified that a few children are at this point, you can then give a second input, explaining to them how to tackle the more challenging task – any children already working on it who have struggled (identified by your in-class, on-the-spot formative assessment) can join in with this group at this point.

Hopefully you get the picture. Your formative assessment can change everything. No more three-way differentiation based on summative assessment from a month ago when you tested them on a completely different unit of work. No more children sitting bored through an explanation of something they already can do. No more children at the other end of the spectrum being totally confounded by a teacher modelling something that they don't have the underpinning basics for yet. Formative assessment which truly informs everything about your lesson from where children sit, to the task they complete, to the time during the lesson when they receive your input.

Teacher Spotlight
Benjamin Barker, Vice Principal at
The King's Leadership Academy, Warrington

Teacher bio-sketch: Ben has been teaching for ten years now, originally working in Runcorn as a science teacher. Following three years for the start his career, he is now embarking on his seventh at King's Leadership Academy in Warrington where he is Vice Principal (Teaching & Learning) as well as Head of Science. Starting at a brand new free school he has experienced a different set of challenges during this time, from – in the early days – creating resources and a curriculum from scratch all the way through to the new GCSEs and Key Stage 5 courses that his academy now offer. Originally from Norfolk, he now calls Liverpool his home with his wife and son Theo. You can find him tweeting at @BenjaminDBarker

We feel that the ability to use both formative and summative assessments in a variety of ways is key in helping our pupils on their journey with us. From brand new King's pupils in Year 7 to, what we hope, will be young women and men with the intellectual habits, qualities of character and scientific literacy to read the subject to a higher level.

We use both formative and summative opportunities in a variety of ways over the course of our different curricula. The formative assessment is used to help staff to alter their pedagogy, resources and activities to help pupils progress through the course. The summative assessment points are used to evaluate how well skills have been developed and knowledge can be recalled.

How do we use formative assessment?

We move through the feedback cycle for the following reasons: to help inform future teaching, to identify gaps in learning or skills, and to help with future planning of lessons. At the start of the term, the staff will divide the knowledge and skills into one of three sections. The first is something that we feel we can assess pupils on with low stakes methods, such as do now quizzes, the second is the material that we think could be assessed by self or peer methods and the final is the knowledge or skills we feel must be marked by the teacher, the subject specialist. An example might be in physics when looking at the practical on specific heat capacity, a relatively complex topic and where the mark schemes are very detailed, convoluted and a well-trained eye is needed. Once we have decided the pieces of work we want teachers to provide feedback for, we then plan which weeks in the term these 'marked' tasks are going to be seen by pupils. For some of them, particularly if we feel we there is opportunity to spiral and/or interleave the learning they might see the *type* of question more than once.

The pupils complete the task, and then the teacher will complete a crib sheet, a form of class marking popularised on social media. This allows staff to reduce the time they spend on the actual task of giving feedback but also allows all pupils to get feedback that is specific to them, see where others may have made mistakes, as well as highlighting where the strengths lie within the collective of the class. As mentioned before, these feedback opportunities will then allow staff to modify their teaching, pedagogy, resource, and so on, accordingly, based on what they have seen in the pupils' work. We also try to delay the completion of these marked tasks. We feel that if a pupil is taught a specific piece of knowledge or a skill, then there is no benefit to giving them a formative task in that same chronological lesson. This, we feel, would be more the pupils performing well (being able to remember what was discussed minutes earlier) as opposed to learning well (being able to recall and reapply the information discussed in lessons prior).

We also try to coach the pupils to leave this formative feedback for their peers. The idea being, if pupils can get better at engaging with a mark scheme and critiquing their peers work, the faster and more embedded the knowledge and skills will be for them. What we have used previously is pre-written formative feedback, allowing pupils to pick the feedback either for themselves or their peers. Over time these comments can be removed or generalised, so that they more closely fit the feedback one would find in an exam mark scheme that our staff are used to using.

How do we use summative assessment?

We use summative assessment more frequently and in a variety of different ways. Starting at the beginning, when pupils move onto a new term, or a new topic, they will be issued with a knowledge organiser – another idea that we saw from teachers on social media and we have taken on board here. The knowledge organiser is split into sections and each one is given to the pupils at a specific time in the future, normally each week. The pupil's task is to learn that portion of the knowledge organiser for a low stakes quiz in a coming lesson. Depending on the year they are in, this could be content covered in the previous lesson, material that is new (flipped approach) or revision of material from a previous term or year. The pupils then take a simple short answer, or even a multiple-choice quiz, as their 'do now' for a future lesson. We also have access to a large bank of questions that covers the entire GCSE specification, we use this for similar reasons, being able to interleave our short answer questions has helped our pupils to do well. The biggest form of summative assessment in terms of marks and time is our mock exams, particularly for our Year 11s. We do these twice over the course of the year and only use past papers. The upside to this is that we can be confident with how well pupils have learnt and recalled the information from the specification as a whole as we can assign a grade to the work. The downside in my mind is that it is likely they will not see similar questions in the real exam. It is because of this we have had to be smart with the feedback we give. Emphasising with pupils that we are less concerned with the fact that would have got a mark, but what was the reason you missed it, for example, do pupils need to be better at recalling physics equations or in the biology paper do they need to be more aware of command words, or possibly in chemistry identifying the number of marks available and setting out answers accordingly. Whatever the response, making pupils better at decoding papers is the key. We spend the weeks following mocks performing gap lessons, that is not being interested in what they got right, but instead, where are the gaps. Staff may do this on a topic-by-topic basis or they might do it based on assessment outcome, what skill, such as data manipulation, are pupils struggling with and how would that change their planning, pedagogy, support and challenge for their pupils?

Chapter review

- Descriptors based on the national curriculum levels were by their very nature far too generic.
- The distorted use of levels for teacher assessments was one of the rationales for the removal of levels.
- The removal of levels has been a step in the right direction, however the reporting of GCSE grades demonstrates that teachers are being asked to provide superficial data that quite simply isn't accurate.
- There needs be a culture shift to modify how assessment is being used in schools for it to be a decisive pedagogy tool that supports the facilitation

of learning, not a term that is used for accountability or to driving school improvement.

- When assessment is formative, the aim is to reveal pupils' weaknesses so that the teacher can act on them. When assessment is summative, the aim is to give pupils a final grade.
- When teachers are being responsive, they could be providing 'in the moment' necessary adjustments to teaching that reflects the data we collect after checking for understanding following knowledge input.

Chapter reflections

The assessment of pupil's learning is widely used by teachers with the main aim of establishing what pupils currently know and what they need to know. Consequently, when it comes to applying assessment practices in the classroom, it is important that we concentrate on using it as a tool to help pupils learn. In the next chapter we will consider how we can move pupils forward after we have checked pupil's understanding and provide target-driven improvements – the F and T of CRAFT.

THE 'F' AND 'T': HOW CAN TEACHERS PROVIDE PUPILS WITH PRECISE FEEDBACK TO FEEDFORWARD?

OLIVER CAVIGLIOLI
@olicav olicav.com

'We all need people who will give us feedback. That's how we improve.' – Bill Gates

Andrea, an NQT, spends many of hours outside her allocated teaching time with pupils to provide detailed written feedback as directed by her school's marking policy. She is expected to mark in detail every couple of weeks, providing pupils with a 'what went well' as well as an 'even better if' comment for an extended piece of writing. The extensive nature of the written feedback that is expected by her school leaders, means her working week often exceeds 50 hours. It becomes a continuous feedback cycle of providing written feedback for pupils, often repeating the same guidance to several pupils. Andrea is a conscientious teacher and wants to be seen doing a good job. The elusive 'book looks' are held on a regular basis, which means she must ensure she keeps on top of her marking. She questions the impact of this extensive written feedback to her pupil outcomes.

When teachers discuss the process of marking, the dread sets in, as it conjures up hours of work that is undertaken daily by teachers of all phases. Understandably, it is a key topic of discussion in the frequent lively debates on the issue of teacher workload. I'm sure that when people sign up to become a teacher there is an acknowledgment that part of the job description will inevitably involve the act of providing feedback to pupils. However, with the number of teaching groups allocated for the average teacher ranging from 5-12 groups, the necessity of school policies to mark every two weeks with written feedback to every pupil, it can understandably become all too consuming, as the marking piles up.

At the end of the school day I used to regularly take a set of books home to keep up with the marking policy, which at that time was to provide feedback for a piece of work every two to three weeks. I would wheel in the trolley cart to transport my class set of books after years of attempting to carry them under my arms for them to either remain in the car or on the dining table. The pressure to keep up to date with the policy often taking its toll. For those teachers that did somehow find the time to keep on top of their marking and provide detailed written feedback, week in week out, they were hailed as teachers who were expert practitioners when it came to marking books. The more detailed and extensive feedback an individual teacher produced, the higher the bar was raised for the rest. Quantity was king over quality. On reflection, keeping on top of 'marking' books merely ticks the box in terms of meeting the expectations of school policies, however just because books look like they have been marked because there's lots of red pen doesn't mean the form of marking being received is contributing towards moving pupils forward in improving outcomes along their learning journey.

The increased national awareness of marking for teacher workload and recruitment retention has led to several government reports and reviews in recent years. In 2016, the Independent Teacher Workload Review Group indicated that the growing emphasis on school policies insisting on frequent and deep written marking had become a significant burden for teachers.

In the report produced in 2016, the review group considered the characteristics of ineffective marking and characterised it as follows:

- It usually involves an excessive reliance on the labour-intensive practices under our definition of deep marking, such as extensive written comments in different colour pens, or the indication of when verbal feedback has been given by adding 'VF' on a pupil's work.
- It can be disjointed from the learning process, failing to help pupils improve their understanding. This can be because work is set and marked to a false timetable and based on a policy of following a mechanistic timetable, rather than responding to pupils' needs.
- It can be dispiriting, for both teacher and pupil, by failing to encourage and engender motivation and resilience.
- It can be unmanageable for teachers, and teachers forced to mark

work late at night and at weekends are unlikely to operate effectively in the classroom.[1]

In the 2019 teacher workload survey, when teachers and middle leaders were asked about time spent on non-teaching tasks in the week, the marking/correcting of pupils' work scored high with minimal difference between the 2016 teacher workload survey. In the primary phase the percentage decreased from 98% to 95%, whilst in the secondary phase the percentage increased from 96% to 97%. When asked about the average hours spent on marking/correcting pupils' work this had increased from 6 to 8.2 hours for primary teachers and 6.3 to 8 hours for secondary teachers.

Clearly, the emphasis on the type of feedback, driven by marking pupil work through written comments, is cultivating the issues that permeate the education sphere when it is mentioned. However, the research suggests that the act of giving feedback to pupils is one of the most effective strategies in contributing towards improving pupil outcomes.

So, how can we move away from an ineffective and inefficient way of providing feedback to a culture where precision feedback is a powerful strategy to support the triangulation between teachers, pupils and parents?

There are several examples of the definition of feedback, Hattie and Timperley outline the meaning: 'Feedback is conceptualised as information provided by an agent (*e.g.* teacher, peer, book, parent, self, experience) regarding aspects of one's performance or understanding.'[2]

The art of giving feedback to pupils is as an important element of the teaching and learning cycle that enables teachers to support pupils in closing the knowledge gap, the discrepancy between what pupils currently know and what pupils need to know. To create an effective feedback culture, I would suggest the following principles would support this:

- **Timely** – in relation to the delivery by teachers and the space for pupils to respond.
- **Receptive culture** – where pupils embrace the process of feedback.
- **Granular** – a concrete and specific target that can be actioned by pupils.
- **Supports self-regulation** – creates conditions for pupils to have clarity in the advice given by teachers and act on it.
- **Fluid process** – flowing between teacher-to-teacher, pupil-to-pupil.

---

1. Department for Education (2016) 'Eliminating Unnecessary Workload Around Marking: Report of the Independent Teacher Workload Review Group'. London: The Stationery Office.
2. Hattie, J. and Clarke, S. (2008) *Visible Learning: Feedback*. Abingdon, Oxon: Routledge.

Whilst the act of providing feedback can be powerful, the variation in its effectiveness can be equally high with Kulhavy indicating that even when feedback is provided it can be accepted, modified, or rejected.[3] Take the example of someone attending a gym class. The gym instructor will advise one of their participants who might not be following the routine correctly, providing verbal feedback on what to do. The way in which this feedback is delivered to the participant and the specific instructions given will have an influence on whether the receiver of the feedback, the participant in their class, chooses to accept and modify their actions or reject and continue to make the same mistakes. The same scenario can happen in the classroom. When a teacher provides pupils with feedback in the lesson pupils may accept, modify or reject the guidance given. When I think back and reflect on some of the scenarios in the classroom, I've experienced from teaching a class myself or observing another colleague, pupils can become defensive about their work when teachers provide them with 'in the moment' feedback.

In a series of meta-analysis from a range of studies conducted, Hattie highlighted the level of variations in the influence of feedback on pupil outcomes. Whilst there were variations in the effect size ranging from -0.04 to 1.24, the studies demonstrated a positive impact on pupil outcomes, with the average effect size from 196 studies 0.79. Consequently, the feedback provided by teachers may not provide enough correcting influence to change or improve pupil's knowledge to close the gap. Hattie and Timperley summarise some of the main reflections based on the outcomes of these studies:

1. Feedback is more effective when it provides information on correct rather than incorrect responses and when it builds on changes from previous trails.
2. The impact of feedback is influenced by the difficulty of goals and tasks. It appears to have the most impact when goals are specific and challenging but task complexity is low.
3. Praise for task performance appears to be ineffective, which is hardly surprising because it contains such little learning-related information.
4. It appears to be more effective when there are perceived low rather than high levels of threat to self-esteem, presumably because low-threat conditions allow attention to be paid to the feedback.[4]

For many years' pupils would chase me down the corridor yearning to know what grade they had got in their test the previous lesson, often a couple of hours

---

3.   Hattie, J. and Timperley, H. (2007) 'The Power of Feedback', *Review of Educational Research* 77 (1) pp. 81-112.
4.   Ibid.

later! I applauded their enthusiasm and commitment to their studies and would inevitably give them their grade when I handed back their piece of work. The room erupted with a buzz of exchanging grades with their peers. Inevitably there would always be several pupils who didn't perform as well as expected and they would sit back and hide behind their test paper. The anxiety would build as the ripples of, 'what did you get?' permeated the room. The focus was on the grade they had been awarded and not the constructive comments I had included regarding their next steps. All too often, as I discussed in Chapter 3, the pupil's performance was related to them being associated with a grade or, in the past, a level. 'I'm a Grade 4 pupil.' The mechanics involved in the labelled outcome were hidden behind the grade awarded. The pupils who hadn't achieved a grade they were happy with, or one they were expected to achieve, would exhibit defensive behaviour and an unwillingness to either accept or engage in the aftermath of the few minutes of grade exchanges. They were shielding themselves from the embarrassment of being labelled with a grade below their peers. Equally, the awarding of a grade often suggests that the learning process has ended, hence the reason why pupils are awarded a grade at the end of their GCSEs and A Level studies.

Butler and Nisan (1986) conducted research to compare the effects of constructive feedback and grades and concluded that when pupils were awarded a grade it resulted in depressed creativity, fostered fear of failure, and weakened students' interest. Butler argued that when teachers provide pupils with information that focuses on themselves, the awarding of a grade, it merely promotes boosting their ego as pupils compare themselves in relation to the achievement of others. On the flip side, when task-specific comments were used there were fewer negative consequences. In a follow up study, Butler (1988) discovered that pupil's performance was enhanced by almost 30% when they received comments specifically tailored to their performance.[5] Further studies conducted yielded similar results with grades having a negative impact on pupils' performance. In addition, the feedback intervention theory suggested by Kluger and DeNisii in 1996, highlighted that when pupils are provided with feedback it should direct their attention to the details of the specific task and the next steps that would assist them in achieving the expected outcomes. Consequently, when teachers provide a grade it can distract them away from the task because it suggests that the task is now finished. We should look to design our learning sequences so that pupils are enriched with regular formative feedback that puts them back on the right track of their learning journey. The grade merely takes them off in the wrong direction, akin to a road with a dead end. Any use of grading or

---

5. Butler, R. (1988) 'Enhancing and undermining intrinsic motivation: The effects of task-involving and ego-involving evaluation on interest and performance', *British Journal of Educational Psychology* 58 (1).

marks should be used infrequently and for internal teacher reference, to avoid the assumption that the learning journey has ended.

Alongside the caution of the use of grades/marks in the feedback process, Carol Dweck a Professor of Psychology at Columbia University conducted research on pupil's motivation, building on the work of others on how humans attribute success and failure, known as the 'attribution theory'.

In the next part of this chapter, I will explore several strategies that teachers could use to approach feedback in the classroom.

The language of feedback

When parents and teachers consider the importance of feedback there is often an assumption that pupils will naturally have a shared commitment to being recipients of the feedback given to them to move them on in their learning journey. However, this is often not the case and if we want pupils to be receptive, we need to create classroom climates where the language of feedback is cultivated to build pupil's resilience to receiving, encoding and processing the advice provided to move them forward. Establish a feedback charter where pupils and teachers embrace the feedback exchange and realise the powerful benefits it has on moving them up the knowledge ladder. This could be related to feedback that is exchanged through teacher to pupil or pupil-to-pupil. If we want pupils to value the feedback given, we must invest in creating a culture where pupils value the feedback.

Equally, we want to ensure that feedback is razor sharp and not illusive in the language used to direct improvement. There were many times in the past when I was guilty of writing comments, like the following: 'Great effort – add more detail to your explanation', or 'Fantastic piece of work – see if you can add more depth to your points.'

These comments are somewhat unhelpful because they are too generic, and it should have been no surprise that pupils needed me to clarify my feedback to advice exactly what I was expecting from them to demonstrate they were 'adding more detail to their explanations'. This delays the effectiveness of feedback provided and the time spent on writing the same ineffective comments on pupil's work. If we want pupils to reflect and respond on feedback, we need to provide pupils with comments that are focused on directing improvements that can be applied across different concepts and processes in your subject. The comments provided should be goal specific and granular. Too many comments on pupil's work could lead to them becoming overwhelmed and not want to engage in responding to the feedback provided.

In English, when pupils are writing an essay the teacher may advice the following:

- Remember to reference the writer when you are introducing a quote.
- Support your points by commenting on the connotation of words and images. For example…
- What connective could you add here to vary the structure of your sentences…?

In geography, when pupils are explaining a concept or process, or using case study evidence a teacher may advice the following:

- When explaining your point link back to the question set. For example,…
- When commenting on a place you have studied use specific facts and figures. For example…

In dance, when pupils are exploring the use of different techniques the teacher may provide the following precise feedback: 'When describing an exercise be specific and say how many times you would repeat it and for how long…'

Secondly, the language of our feedback will be dependent on whether we are checking knowledge recall or application of knowledge. When teachers are checking for understanding relating to the recall of concepts and processes, the feedback will be targeted to clarifying misconceptions, or gaps in understanding of these core aspects of knowledge for a subject. For example, in geography, pupils regularly have a misconception related to the concept of urbanisation, often suggesting that it is the increase in the number of people living in urban areas. Feedback would be directed at clarifying and dispelling the misconception the following lesson or during the lesson when spotting the error whilst pupils are in the process of learning. On the other hand, the language of feedback can be associated with pupil's application of knowledge. For example, when explaining concepts and processes in geography, pupils should make a point, develop that point and then provide a linking sentence to support the point that they have made. The language of feedback in this instance would be to reaffirm how pupils should apply knowledge and is 'mobile', in the sense that it applies to their application of other disciplines within the subject. Reducing the need for the frequency of this feedback, and consequently a focus on dispelling misconceptions could be to provide cue cards and prompts to support in scaffolding the expectations related to applying knowledge.

The relentless approach

Consistency is key. When you have established a feedback culture in your classroom and the wider school, it's important to maintain the approach and be consistent in your application. Every subject is unique, and it would be counterproductive for school leaders to insist on a one-size-fits-all approach to providing feedback. In Ofsted's myth busting report of 2015, there was a clear indication for all teachers that there were no expectation to see any specific type or frequency that teachers provide to pupils. Consequently, we can feel empowered to decide on the most effective feedback approaches for our pupils. If we can create the right conditions for pupils to receive feedback, it will go a long way in breaking down the barriers to pupils accepting the feedback we provide and then using this to 'feedforward' into future learning. For example, let's consider the challenges posed by an obstacle course. The greater the number of obstacles on the course, the longer the potential finish time as you work to avoid and overcome the obstacles that are in the way. The fewer obstacles we put in front of our pupils, the greater the chance they will be able to complete the course more efficiently. As a result, the more consistent we are in our approach to feedback, the greater the chance of pupil's being successful.

When pupils are working to construct a graph in geography it is expected that they will have a clear title, labelled their axes and drawn the graph in pencil. Reminding pupils of this success criteria at every opportunity when completing this type of task will support in reducing cognitive load, and with repetition, become more proficient in completing a graph with these key requirements completed, reducing the need for further guidance in the future. Practice makes permanent. Collaboration with other departments who work to develop similar skills within subjects, like the success criteria for constructing a graph, will also support pupils in reducing variability in expectations, and thus the directed feedback required from teachers.

In dance, when pupils are mastering a routine, they are required to demonstrate a range of expressive skills during their performance. Pupils receive consistent verbal feedback throughout the construction of their performance to support them in developing its complexity. Pupils are reminded of the following key components that will be crucial to support their performance: musicality, focus facial expression, spatial awareness, projection, phrasing, sensitivity to other dancers, and communication of choreographic intent. It is expected that pupils will use these skills across their difference styles of dance with teachers remind them to use these expressive skills through regular and consistent language of feedback.

Actions

Delaying the marks/grades

After pupils have completed test, mark their work as usual but delay awarding any marks or grades on their completed work. This will be important in reducing the distraction that these numbers create, indicated by the research we discussed earlier.

Using a whole-class feedback sheet, make a note of any common misconceptions/errors that may have arisen to discuss with pupils the following lesson. In the following lesson, hand back their test ready to annotate with any of the misconceptions/errors. The emphasis here is on the pupils doing the work and not you as the teacher. An example of a feedback sheet provided to pupils is illustrated below. Pupils re-draft on the aspects that are in the 'R' and 'A' of the sheet.

They use the next step box to focus their re-drafting and focus on the next steps to feedforward into next stage of learning where they may be asked to apply similar knowledge or skill in a different scenario. We want pupils to not make the same error or report a misconception.

There are times where it might be necessary to re-teach a concept or process if most of the class didn't perform well on before they embark on re-drafting. In *Slow Teaching*, Jamie Thom unpicks how teachers can find calm, clarity and impact in the classroom. Taking the time to re-teach a concept or process that pupils didn't grasp is an important part of closing the feedback loop. We should not worry about slowing down the teaching sequence and finding the time to ensure pupils understand before moving them along the learning journey.

Feedback Sheet – Changing Cities/ Weather & Climate

Create a series of models that you could use to analyse and unpick the response to demonstrate how it achieves excellence. In this part of the feedback cycle its important to give pupils the chance to reflect on their own next steps, time to process the feedback given. We need to give them ample time to reflect on the feedback and make improvements to their work through re-drafting. During this process, it's important to monitor their re-drafts to ensure they are acting upon the feedback given.

At the end of the feedback process, give pupils the opportunity to reflect on the revision strategies they used in preparation for the test and for them to consider the ones that they may adopt next time.

The final part of the process is for pupils to take their paper home with the feedback sheet to have the dialogue with home, something I passionately believe is an important element in the learning process, something I discussed earlier on in Chapter 2. If we are to successfully CRAFT learning, the involvement of parents in supporting and guiding pupils along their journey is crucial. As teachers we should create as many opportunities as possible to triangulate involvement with home. A completed sheet illustrating the feedback from a parent is below. Creating this connection with home reinforces the importance of the feedback process to pupils and raises the bar for them to aspire to achieve their best, so that they can celebrate their successes with home. When parents evening arrives, this will elicit a productive conversation around their child's progress which they will have been party to throughout the academic year.

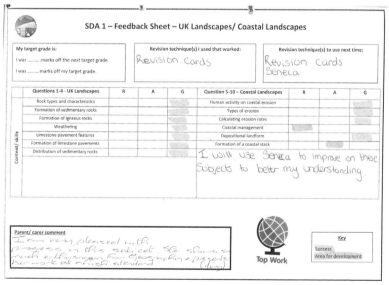

When providing feedback on knowledge recall questions, ones where there is a right or wrong answer, having pupils mark themselves and gain instant feedback can be beneficial. There are times when it is appropriate to delay the feedback and there are times when the delay in the feedback may not be necessary. In the example knowledge grid below, pupils indicate the degree of success in answering the questions set through a pit stop review of concepts or processes taught in a learning sequence.

KNOWLEDGE REVIEW

I can state the impacts of coastal erosion on people.
I know how one of these impacts can have ripple effects.
I know the effects of coastal flooding on people.
I can recognise mass movement processes.
I know the definition of and examples of coastal management.
I can recognise the purpose of coastal management strategies.
I know the advantages and disadvantages of coastal management strategies.
I know the reasons why the Holderness coastline is vulnerable to erosion and flooding.
I can recognise transportation processes.
I know different types of sedimentary rocks.
I know what influences the shape of spits.
I know the feature found with a coastal bar.

NEXT STEPS
1. Complete an assignment on SENECA to review your understanding of core knowledge.
2. Create a revision card on the area of core knowledge that you were unable to accurately recall.
3...

'In the moment' feedback

Verbal feedback that occurs in the stages of knowledge acquisition and application is a powerful feedback tool. In Jack Tavassoly-Marsh's teacher spotlight at the end of this chapter, he provides a glimpse into the use of visualisers to deliver verbal feedback. When pupils are applying knowledge, circulate the room and monitor their performance towards the learning outcomes. Use this opportunity to direct pupils whilst they are in the moment to enhance their learning to reduce misconceptions or mistakes setting in that you will need to rectify the following lesson. When pupils are practicing, we want to re-direct any errors 'in the moment' to reduce errors or misconceptions settling in that could be more difficult to reverse later.

Take the following examples of question stems that could be used when circulating the room to monitor pupil's practice mode. Focus on thought provoking questions that focus on the performance of the work and not that specifically of the pupil.

'Tom, that's an excellent quote to support your point on how the character is portrayed in the play. Can you develop that further to specify why this quote supports your point...?'

'Lucy, I can see that you have made a point about a cause of globalisation. Can you develop the point to explain why it has contributed towards this concept....?'

'Ryan, can you give me an example of what you mean...?'

'Abigail, do you think you could support that point you have made with a fact or several statistics...?'

The error detective

We want our pupils to be masters of their own learning where they can self-regulate their progress along the intended learning journey. Creating a feedback culture where pupils know there is an expectation that part of the learning process is for them to check their work prior to submission can ensure we receive work that goes a long way to meeting our high expectations. This allows you as the teacher to focus on identifying the granular feedback to close the knowledge gap. I have spent many of hours writing the same comments on work that could have been rectified if pupils had proofread their own work before submission. Equally, this will reduce the feedback required and focus on next steps that are granular and knowledge driven.

At the beginning, pupils will inevitably struggle to check their work, and this will require patience and support to enable them to become more effective in this process. In the first instance, support pupils in checking their own work by providing them with clear success criteria that outlines what excellence looks like. Secondly, give them enough time to proofread their work during the lesson. Thirdly, insist that pupils do this every time they are due to submit a piece of work for you to review. Be relentless in your expectations and insist on 'attention to detail' to enable them to achieve the highest of expectations. Finally, remind pupils of the importance of your time in marking their work. You want them to understand that you want the feedback to be focused on moving their learning forward and not responding to unnecessary mistakes. Ultimately, as I mentioned at the start of this chapter, feedback is a two-way process. Pupils should be aware of their important role in ensuring this process is effective in supporting them to become more proficient pupils within the disciplines of our subjects.

In the final part of this chapter the spotlights are on Zoe Enser, Sarah Larsen and Jack Tavassoly-Marsh who share an insight into how they have approached target-driven feedback in their own classroom and schools.

Teacher Spotlight
Zoe Enser, Lead Advisor for
The Education People

Teacher bio-sketch: Zoe Enser is Lead English Advisor for The Education People in Kent. This follows 20 years in the classroom, 11 years as a head of english and three years leading on CPD. You can find her tweeting at @greeborunner

Feedback and marking has always been a hot topic amongst teachers, especially English teachers. It is easy to spend hours and hours correcting every mistake made and writing lengthy comments for students to simply ignore the advice and repeat the errors in later work. Worse still the more they repeat this the more likely it is that errors become embedded and misconceptions are retained over important information. I am sure I am not the only teacher who has checked spelling corrections in a book to discover that a student has rewritten the word five times with the same error repeated over and again. This is both frustrating and tiring for all.

Making time in the lessons to ensure that students are acting upon your hard work is therefore essential but can be time consuming. That's fine as long as that time is having the impact desired and this is where a policy of 'feedforward' becomes invaluable.

Unlike 'feedback' which focuses on improving the work a student produced, valuable when refining a piece in the drafting process, but less useful when they will be encountering a whole new question or text, feedforward focuses on improving the learning of the students.

In my classroom this is done using a two-pronged process; the first is about giving students the opportunity to reflect on the work they have produced, exploring errors and practising getting it right. The second is about my planning and how I feedforward into what the students are going to learn in their subsequent lessons and terms.

In the first stage students are encouraged to think about their work met cognitively. I support them with whole class feedback or individual comments to identify their own errors, gaps and areas for improvement. This may also include sharing exemplar responses or looking at ways to improve a specific example, as well as looking at their own work.

Once they have had an opportunity to reflect on this and have a clear understanding on ways their work could be improved, students are given a task to consolidate this. For example, if we have been looking at writing about language – a key skill for GCSE – we would then look at another text and practise embedding improvements in this new task. A short conversation with a group of girls in my class a few years ago highlighted the importance of this, as when asked during a DIRT task what they would do if they attempted this task again, they could only talk about how they would improve that one example. They couldn't imagine how they would transfer this feedback into a new task, so I ensure that I help them to bridge this gap by giving them a scaffold to do just that.

The second, and in my view most important part of feedforward, is about what I do with the information from their assessments in the weeks and months that follow. When I read over their books and assessments, I am looking for where there might be gaps in knowledge which I need to fill. I am looking to see what they can do confidently and what they need to revisit again. I then plan opportunities for this, using retrieval practice to make learning stick in their schema, reinforcing it with further opportunities to practise using that information and consolidate the process.

All of the information I gather as I mark is fed forward into the next scheme, even if we are looking at a completely different text. Learning from *Macbeth* is reinforced as we look at power and conflict poems, the morality aspects in *A Christmas Carol* and the conventions of drama texts in *An Inspector Calls*. Equally if we are looking at students producing their own texts, I would give them some immediate feedback which they could reflect on, including identifying some of their own frequent errors. I would then give them a chance to look at some good examples that we would unpick together. Then they would complete a further task to practice those skills again. I will make sure that in the subsequent lessons across the rest of the term or year, I make opportunities to revisit this though as I want the learning to really stick.

Every time I mark students' work I am focusing on those next steps I need to feedforward into their work and into my planning. This helps to support learning that is less transient and is centred on the principle of improving the pupil and not the work.

Teacher Spotlight
Sarah Larsen,
Geography teacher at Reigate School

Teacher bio-sketch: Sarah has been a geography teacher in and around Greater London for 22 years. Prior to having her first child, she led the geography department at her current school for just over a year. She is passionate about being research-informed in her teaching and has spent the last two years devoting much to her reading and networking around reducing written marking and increasing her use of immediate, verbal feedback. In 2018, she was one of the 13 teachers who carried out research for UCL and Ross McGill's 'Verbal Feedback Project', launching the report in September of that year. She has spoken at several educational events about the merits of verbal feedback including ResearchED Surrey and TMGeogIcons. You can find her tweeting at @sarahlarsen74

My journey with verbal feedback and the move away from extensive written comments in books began at the start of 2018. It was at this time that my school was looking to make the move away from written marking in books. We had begun the change by realising that not every page needed comments and grades, but that some pieces of work still needed detailed feedback. We were, however, still initialling every page in their books in order to acknowledge that the work had been done. Yet even this practice was still relatively time consuming, and, we were gradually realising, added nothing to student learning. My Senior Leadership Team (SLT) were keen to move forward even further to reduce workload and to improve outcomes for students.

At this time, I happened to chance upon Victoria Hewitt's (@MrsHumanities on social media) whole class verbal feedback sheet on Twitter, which can be seen below.

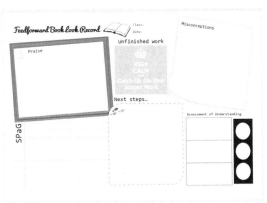

She and others were using this method to give verbal feedback after a class had attempted a substantial piece of class work, homework or assessment. The sheets negated the need on the part of the teacher for laboriously writing out the same comments 30 times over, which many students wouldn't understand fully or be able to act upon, resulting in the same errors being made the next time they attempted a similar piece of work. What they *did* allow the teacher to do – by projecting it onto their classroom screen the next time they saw their students and returned their work to them – was to make them *think*. As Daniel Willingham states in his book *Why Don't Students Like School?*, 'memory is the residue of thought'. In other words, when students are made to think hard about something, it is more likely to stick so that they are less likely to make the same mistakes next time. With our SLT's permission, our humanities department set about trialling this method.

A completed version of a whole class verbal feedback sheet can be seen below.

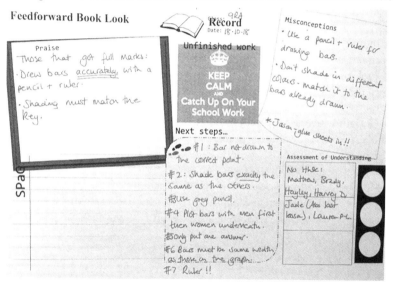

There is space on the sheet for the teacher to record spelling errors, common misconceptions, names or examples of good pieces of work, and the traffic light section that can remain hidden to students for the teacher to record the names of students who are not quite where they should be yet. One of the key features, however, is the 'next steps' box at the bottom that allows the teacher to record a series of codes and areas for improvement. Doubtlessly, these comments would previously have been written out many times over the course of marking a set of books, homework or assessments. The corresponding code(s) are also only written on each student's work. Students can then copy out each statement onto their work and each code is explained and perhaps correct answers modelled as part of the time allocated by the teacher for improvement.

However, what is crucial in all of this is the time given over to the teacher verbally explaining and *showing* their students how to improve, along with reflection and improvement time for the students. Comments such as 'more detail needed' are meaningless unless they are shown what an answer with more detail might look like. If the teacher can live model an excellent answer, talking through each step they take whilst they do so as if they were the student, then this is where verbal feedback can really start to take effect. It is imperative that time is allocated for the feedback to be acted upon and improvements made to their piece of work, having been made to think hard about what it is that they need to do in order to improve. Examples of improvements to work can be seen below – in this case, part of a Year 10 student's assessment. In the first example, the student has not only drawn on the correct answer, but has made a note to herself about *why* this answer is correct, demonstrating that she has thought about this concept, thus making it more likely that she will remember when attempting a similar question in the future.

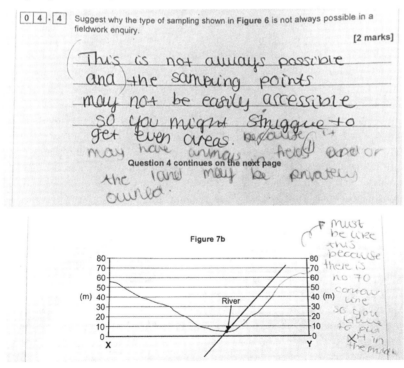

Figure 7b

Verbal feedback can also be carried out whilst the students are working in a lesson, and this is another method that more and more staff at Reigate School are beginning to use. Provided that the key elements for success have been shared with a class, and are visible to students, along with, perhaps all or part of a model answer having been modelled first then hidden by the teacher (again, visualisers are ideal for this), the teacher is then able to circulate whilst students are working. Sometimes, this may involve as little as circling or highlighting an incorrect element of their work (remember that we want the student to *think* about what they need to do to improve, not just for them to be passively told), or pausing to ask the student to consider what might need improving. I know some teachers who like to use colour-coded stickers too. This can take a bit of practice – ensuring that there is enough time to get around to all students and that behaviour is good enough to do so, for example. However, if the reasons for giving feedback this way are shared with the students, I have found it far easier to obtain students' buy-in. Another element that is important to consider is that if I see the same mistakes being made by several students in the class, rather than stating the same thing several times to different individuals, I stop the class and address that misconception or even reteach that concept.

A third method of verbal feedback that I have found to be particularly useful and which I have been using for at least a year now is live marking under my visualiser. As part of a class survey for Ross McGill and UCL's Verbal Feedback Project which I was involved in (see Ross' Teacher Toolkit blog for a download-able copy of the final report), students seemed to favour this method the most. They told me that it gave them immediate feedback and showed them what a good piece of work looked like, so that they could make improvements in the moment rather than two weeks later once their books had been marked using written marking. In fact, my classes are so used to this process happening most lessons that some students will now ask if their work can be placed under the visualiser before I have had a chance to ask anyone! Whilst circulating, I will choose a student's book to use for the live marking – often not the best piece as I want my class to think about what improvements could be made to that piece in order to aid them with the same thought processes about their own.

The piece of work is projected onto the class screen using the visualiser and I read the work through, picking out and ticking the good points whilst explaining what is good about it. However, I also invite the class to tell me what improvements could be made. For example, 'how could this idea have been expressed using a greater range of geographical vocabulary?' or 'how could this point be extended further?' I will annotate the improvements for the class to see. At this stage, their pens should be down. Many will be tempted to simply copy what I have written onto their work, instead they should be being made to *think* about why this piece of work is good and/or needs the improvements that are shown. As with the other methods, time then needs to be built in after this stage so that students can improve their work. There are the inevitable hands that shoot straight up with requests for help, 'Miss, what do I need to do to improve mine?', but I always encourage the students to think about this for themselves first, as this is more likely to result in them *remembering* how to produce a good piece of work next time around. The example below shows the work of a Year 7 student on the SEND register with low prior attainment, who, after a term of benefiting from seeing live marking, produced by far his best, most well-structured piece of work to date, having been made to think about what a good piece of geographical writing should contain on several previous occasions. Whilst not perfect, he has begun to demonstrate that ideas need to be expanded upon and that lists are unacceptable. He has taken care with punctuation and presentation and included specific details about named animals and other key facts and figures, all of which I have modelled and discussed during live marking sessions on several previous occasions.

With all these methods, it is imperative that we see the purpose of verbal feedback as beyond simply improving that particular piece of work. Rather, it should encourage the students to see this as part of a bigger picture of moving towards excellence and mastery of our subjects so that each time they attempt a similar piece of work, they do so with improved outcomes. Feedback needs to cause thinking for this to happen and time must be planned in for students to reflect on their work and to decide, after teacher guidance and modelling, what improvements they need to make. As with any changes to classroom practice, 'retraining' students to think in this way will take time, but the rewards for their outcomes are, without a doubt, worth the effort.

Teacher Spotlight
Jack Tavassoly-Marsh,
Vice Principal of Farnham Heath End

Teacher bio-sketch: Jack is a geography teacher and was head of geography for four years, prior to taking up the role of assistant headteacher, with the primary responsibility of ITT and NQT to NQT+3 teacher development. Jack now leads teaching and learning across the school and the school's aim is to become research-informed in all that they do, as teachers, in the classroom. Jack is also the organiser of ResearchED Surrey and has done consultancy work with geography departments across the south east as an SLE. Jack is speaking at ResearchED events across the subject this year, as well as at the Festival of Education. Jack's main aim is to ensure that all classrooms are truly inclusive and that teachers understand how they can be more effective than they already are, whilst always improving his own teaching too. You can find him tweeting at @GeogMarsh

I hate to admit it, but I stood up in front of colleagues in 2014 and emphasised the need to create a dialogue with students when marking. At the time the school had a marking policy whereby a targeted piece of work should be marked for every student, in every subject, every two weeks. We promoted triple marking. That was, for a teacher to mark the work, followed by students writing a response to the written marking from the teacher, with the teacher then writing a written response to the student. This created great dialogue and an understanding of where each individual needed to improve, or so we thought....

What actually happened was that teachers burnt out trying to adhere to the timescale of the policy, and teachers kept writing the same thing on many occasions, spending hours on end doing so. The focus was on marking and not planning to teach the content the most effective way the first time around. It

THE 'F' AND 'T'

was utter madness. It is my biggest regret in my teaching career and led us, as a school, on the path to research-informed practice, working out what works or what is most likely to work, having reviewed the evidence available.

Luckily, the triple marking didn't last long (a term or so), and in 2016 the Education Endowment Foundation released their report on written marking entitled 'A marked improvement?'. The report was a game changer. It made it clear that written marking, as we had introduced, was pretty flawed.

Here are some of the major findings of that report:

- Careless mistakes should be marked differently to errors resulting from misunderstanding. The latter may be best addressed by providing hints or questions that lead pupils to underlying principles – the former by simply marking the mistake as incorrect, without giving the right answer.
- Awarding grades for every piece of work may reduce the impact of marking, particularly if pupils become preoccupied with grades at the expense of a consideration of teachers' formative comments.
- The use of targets to make marking as specific and actionable as possible is likely to increase pupil progress.
- Pupils are unlikely to benefit from marking unless some time is set aside to enable pupils to consider and respond to marking.
- Some forms of marking, including acknowledgement marking, are unlikely to enhance pupil progress. A mantra might be that schools should mark less in terms of the number of pieces of work marked, but mark better.

In school, the focus then shifted towards whole-class feedback. Reading student work and jotting down common misconceptions, careless mistakes and areas of strength, along with spelling of key vocabulary for that subject. Whilst this process markedly reduced teacher workload, and provided the same level of feedback for students, there was still a sense that it wasn't the most effective form of feedback. This is due to the time between the students completing the work and the feedback being given back to them. Even if that was the next lesson, there could be anywhere between 1 to 20 lessons in between the two events. There would always be a day between the two as a minimum the way our timetable works. Practically, this meant that students would have a high chance of forgetting a lot of their thought process that they were going through during the task, when the feedback was being given. Lessons where feedback was being given thus needed to go back and get students back into the 'zone' of thinking about what they were thinking about at the time they completed the task.

Subsequently, we shifted focus to live feedback, and live modelling prior to the task, to try and give each students the best chance of producing their best effort in that specific moment, when they are thinking hard about the task in hand. As a school, we read widely around providing feedback to students.

- *What Does This Look Like In The Classroom: Bridging The Gap Between Research And Practice* by Carl Hendrick and Robin Macpherson
- *Embedded Formative Assessment* by Dylan Wiliam
- *Making Every Lesson Count* by Shaun Allison and Andy Tharby

From the extensive reading, we decided a move towards live feedback was the way forward.

How did we go about introducing live target-driven feedback?

We purchased visualisers for every classroom at Farnham Heath End School (FHES) and we focused our teacher training on using them confidently to model their thinking when completing tasks, modelling success criteria within exemplar work and providing live feedback on student work in the lesson. We also spent time training teachers to provide the feedback during the task, as well as at the end of the task, so to allow students to produce their best work. An example of this is live modelling the first paragraph of writing silently in front of the class, followed by modelling a second paragraph whilst questioning the students as to what content should be included and how it should be structured. Lastly, the students then complete a paragraph by themselves in silence. At the end of the paragraph, student exemplars are shown, with live feedback given to the class, prior to further writing being undertaken by students.

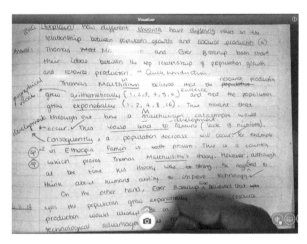

In this photograph, I am giving live feedback, through annotating a student's work underneath the visualiser, against success criteria that was shared with the students. The first paragraph was given live feedback, before the student then worked on further paragraphs, working on the feedback given.

The 'I, We, You' modelling approach is one that we have followed, as a school, as well as completing worked examples, or unpacking worked examples, explaining our thinking. We have found that this allows students to see the feedback given to them 'in the moment', and they can they make the necessary edits/adaptations to their work there and then, when they are thinking about that piece of work. Student engagement has improved in the tasks, as work can be shown at random under the visualiser.

What has been interesting is the movement away from grades at FHES and towards what individual students can and can't do well. Live feedback has been a large part of this process. Before completing tasks, teachers ask students to go back and look at the last time they completed a similar task. What were the areas for improvement last time? What were the strengths? This allows students to start the task with a focus on what they need to improve upon. We look back at completed tasks to then feed forward into the current task.

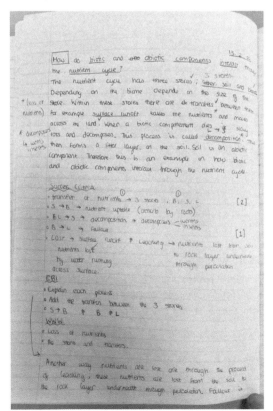

In this photograph, the student has identified where they have met the success criteria in the answer. This was done after live feedback was given under the visualiser to a peer. Under the visualiser, the student completed the piece of work whilst the rest of the class did the same to their work, with this student's work providing guidance to others.

One visual way that this has been implemented in the geography department is through the colour-coding of specific elements of written answers. This allows students to see a visual representation of the different areas of their answer, for example, where they have made simple points, where they have developed those points, and where they have linked their points back to the original question. Through doing this under the visualiser with an exemplar answer, the teacher shows the students what they are looking for to improve their written content and structure. Students then complete the colour-coding on their own answer and get to visually see areas of strength and development. This is effective at the time, but also effective to go back to when doing the next similar task, to provide the student with the area of focus feeding forward.

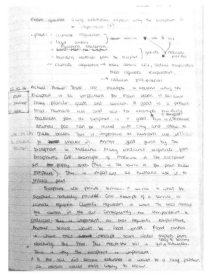 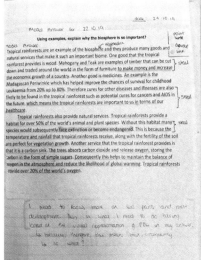

In the photograph on the right, after modelling this live under the visualiser, students' colour-coded a model answer, focusing on points, development of points and links back to the question. In the photograph on the left, the student then applied this to their own answer, and then wrote out what they needed to focus on as a target for next time we write a similar style of written response.

As well as using visualisers, we have had a strong focus on questioning, and specifically using questioning strategies to assess understanding. I won't spend time writing about them here, but we have focused on several strategies from *Teach Like A Champion* by Doug Lemov. We have focused on the following and

I would strongly advise reading about them and how they increase expectations, challenge and assess understanding in lessons:

- Wait time
- No opt-out
- Cold call
- Right is right
- Format matters

Student voice has been immensely positive around being able to improve their work immediately in lessons; along with having teachers explain their thinking and the steps/stages involved prior to the task. Students have a far clearer understanding of success criteria, and a focus on what they can do well and what they need to work on.

FHES student voice:

'I really like watching a teacher explain their thinking whilst going through a task under the visualiser, it gives me confidence to know the steps or stages to go through when it is my turn.' – Year 11 student

'I no longer have to wait for feedback on whether my work is right or wrong, which means my confidence has improved, as I know where improvements are needed straight away.' – Year 11 student

'Having feedback in the lesson on the task means that I can change my work straight away and I know I have been successful and more on track to reach my targets.' – Year 8 student

'I didn't like the thought of my work being shown under the visualiser at first, but now it is happening in most lessons. We get to see how other classmates approach their writing. I have found it specifically useful in English lessons.' – Year 10 student

'Seeing a teacher give live feedback on someone's work under the visualiser, allows us to reflect on our work there and then, making changes straight away. I then know I am on the right track with my work.' – Year 9 student

'I love seeing a teacher explain the steps in a maths calculation under the visualiser, it makes it easier for me to do my calculations afterwards.' – Year 7 student

Chapter review

- Marking has become an unnecessary burden on teacher's time.
- Books with lots of red pen in them doesn't mean the feedback is moving pupils forward.
- The growing emphasis on school policies insisting on frequent and deep written marking had become a significant burden for teachers.
- The act of giving feedback to pupils is one of the most effective strategies in contributing towards improving pupil outcomes.
- Pupils may accept, modify or even reject the feedback we give them depending on the circumstances in which it is delivered.
- The use of grades/marks distracts the learning process, a focus on target-specific comments that direct improvements is more effective in closing the knowledge gap.
- The use of grades or marks should be deployed infrequently to avoid the assumption that the learning journey has ended.
- Feedback is more effective when it provides information on correct rather than incorrect responses and when it builds on changes from previous trails.

Chapter reflections

The act of giving feedback to pupils is a vital element of the learning process and when done effectively can support pupils in establishing the difference between what they know, what they should know, and feeding forward into future learning episodes to close the knowledge gap. In the past, there have been blurred lines between marking and feedback, with marking often the king, becoming an unsustainable and ineffective process for teachers and pupils. Moving forward, we should be empowered to employ a range of written and verbal feedback strategies (individual, peer, self and whole class) that are aligned to the needs of your pupils that dispels the negative connotations of marking that has permeated schools and classrooms. In the final chapter we will consider how leaders can cultivate a culture that CRAFTs learning.

5

THE CRAFT COACH: HOW CAN WE ESTABLISH A CULTURE OF LEARNING?

OLIVER CAVIGLIOLI
@olicav olicav.com

'Culture is the arts elevated to a set of beliefs.'

For many years there has been a growing emphasis that learning is defined by what teachers do or don't do and that pupils behave when learning is 'engaging'. I would argue that this belief is flawed and to grow a culture of learning, there needs to be a collective belief in school communities that the triangulation between teachers, pupils and parents is crucial for a successful learning culture. The responsibilities to create the right conditions for learning to flourish should not lie solely at the feet of teachers.

Fullan (2007) defined a school culture as 'the guiding beliefs and expectations evident in the way a school operates'. Fullan along with other researchers, believed that for schools to develop a positive culture of learning, there needs to be a collaborative approach to the values, beliefs, norms and preferred behaviours.

One aspect for embedding a culture of learning, something Sam Strickland outlines in his spotlight at the end of this chapter is investing in teacher development. The professional development of staff is a vital element to developing a positive culture of learning in schools. We want teachers to feel supported, empowered and develop into consciously competent practitioners that continually reflect on how they can support every pupil to succeed.

Consider the following scenario when providing teachers with feedback to develop their practice in the classroom:

'You need to have more clarity in how you explain ideas to students.'

'You need to work on improving your presence in the classroom.'

'You need to question students more.'

There have been many occasions in the past when this was the type of feedback, I received from people observing my lessons. It was very frustrating to receive such feedback after believing the lesson had gone well, often wondering, what does 'more clarity' mean when explaining? What does 'having more presence' look like in the classroom? Why do I need to question students more? How do I question students more?

This type of feedback can leave you feeling disheartened and not 'good enough' by not providing specific support in what to do next.

All too often the feedback and advice given to teachers lack precise meaning that cannot be actioned, leading to limited improvement in teacher practice and ultimately student outcomes.

This is where the use of instructional coaching when embedding the CRAFT of learning can be implemented to move away from traditional observations and contribute to improving teacher's professional development. In 2018, Sam Sim went as far as saying instructional coaching is currently the best-evidenced form of CPD. Sim defines instructional coaching as follows: 'Instructional coaching involves an expert teacher working with a novice in an individualised, classroom-based, observation-feedback-practice cycle.'

One of the examples of several pieces of evidence that supports his claim is a randomised controlled trial from the My Teaching Partner (MTP) intervention, which demonstrated improved secondary school results in the state of Virginia by an effect size of 0.22, where pupils were taught by teachers who had made the greatest amount of progress from their coaching sessions. This was further supported by a replicated experiment in 2015 where similar positive results were recorded.

In *Get Better Faster*, Paul Bambrick-Santoyo outlines a six-step instructional coaching model that focuses on getting 'granular' by breaking down the feedback teachers receive into one clear highest leverage action step.

Just like a football coach might focus on practising one technique, like short passes, in this model the teaching coach focuses on working with that teacher on one skill at a time. For example, it might be that the coach identifies the overall aim for the teacher observed is to develop the culture of learning in their classroom. Firstly, the coach would break this down into smaller bite-sized action steps so that the teacher can master one skill at a time. In order to master this skill, the coach would provide time for the teacher to practise this skill before delivering it to students in a lesson. After all, teaching is a performance and like any West End actor, practice is crucial. At this stage, the coach may use video of the teacher to help support development. The coach would then follow up on the implementation of the bite-sized action step with the teacher. In this scenario, the coach may spend several weeks or a half term with the teacher supporting them in mastering each skill that ultimately aims to improve the culture of learning in the classroom.

Whilst the evidence for instructional coaching is positive, the implementation of it by school leaders is crucial to ensure it helps teachers to grow. This is outlined by Lucy Steiner and Julie Kowal from the Centre for Comprehensive School Reform and Improvement.

'For an instructional coaching program to be effective, school leaders need to play an active role in selecting trained coaches, developing a targeted coaching strategy, and evaluating whether coaches are having the desired impact on teaching and learning.'

Consequently, there needs to be a clear vision for a school's instructional coaching program, with skilful coaches who work with individual teachers over time. When this is done successfully, it removes the lack of clarity in feedback given to teachers and provides greater collaboration amongst colleagues that ultimately will bring out improvements in teacher practice and student outcomes.

In the final spotlight, Sam Strickland outlines how under his leadership, he has created a culture of learning where the aspects of CRAFT can flourish to support pupils along their learning journey to be successful.

Teacher Spotlight
Sam Strickland, Principal at
The Duston School

Teacher bio-sketch: Sam is the principal of a large all-through school and has helped to guide its GCSE results from the bottom 20% nationally to the top 20% and A Level outcomes to the top 5% nationally. Sam began his teaching career as a history teacher in Bedfordshire having completed his PGCE in secondary history at the University of Cambridge under Christine Counsell. His career quickly accelerated and he became head of history and classics. He then moved on to become a lead professional and worked for a SCITT Consortium. During his time as an assistant head, he had responsibility for the sixth form and led a post 16 consortium arrangement. In 2015 Sam served as an associate principal, with GCSE and A Level results under his tenure receiving commendation from the DFE, Nick Gibb and the SSAT. Sam then served as a vice principal, where he directly oversaw student care, the sixth form, the curriculum and served as the safeguarding lead for an entire trust. The organiser of ResearchED Northampton, Sam is a leading voice in the current conversation in education. He has had educational resources and research published has also delivered courses nationally and served as a lead facilitator for NPQSL. You can find him tweeting at @Strickomaster

What is culture? What is an ethos? What does a school really feel like? Does culture really eat strategy for breakfast? Or do you need a strategy to establish a culture?

Any school leadership course will usually commence with exploring what the differences between leadership and management are. Then delve into the vision, values and ethos of a school. All too often delegates will be told that culture eats strategy for breakfast. However, this is a bit of a chicken and egg syndrome, where you cannot have one without the other.

I would argue that in the first instance you need to have a clear sense of what you want your school culture to be. To clearly know in your own mind what the halcyon dream looks like. When I think about schools, I think of two key components; namely the mother ship, the actual school as a whole and the satellites, which are all of the sub-areas that make up the school (for example, key departmental areas). In some schools the culture is very firmly dictated by the mother ship and permeates explicitly through all the satellites. In other schools the mother ship feels disconnected. In the very worst of examples the satellites can fight it out in a polycratic and disparate style approach, with a strong sense of self help prevalent.

If we are truly to build a culture, then I would suggest that undertaking the following steps are key.

Know what you want and bring people with you

The best piece of advice I was ever given as I became a senior leader for the first time was that leadership is not about you but about everyone else. This has stuck with me throughout my career. Once you know, within yourself, what the halcyon dream is for your school, I would then meet with every single member of staff, with governors, trustees, parents and pupils. Gauge a feeling and view from them regarding what your school is like (assuming you have just started in a new one), what the strengths of the school are and what needs developing and working on. More importantly, share with these people your vision for the school. This is incredibly important in bringing people with you.

You promote what you permit, you permit what you promote

Any school culture will be defined by the behaviour within it. Be very clear, argu-ably explicitly clear, as to what behaviour you will permit, what behaviour you will promote, what behaviour you do not want. Think carefully about the lines in the sand that you will not condone. How you will use rewards, punitive sanctions, praise, rewards, and so on. What emphasis will you place on manners, oracy and routines? Will you treat behaviour as a subject and, therefore, teach it or will you leave it to chance? You also need to consider carefully how you communicate your vision, rules, routines, and so on, to every single stakeholder and how you train people in them. Your biggest marketing tool for your school will be the behaviour of your pupils. This will heavily influence which parents want to send their child to your school, whether staff want to remain in your employment and whether prospective employees will even consider working for you.

Curriculum: Intent and implementation

Think very carefully, very hard, very long and very deep how you want your curriculum to look. I would argue you should spend a huge amount of your time on this. Think carefully, with subject leads, about how you want your curriculum designed and how long you spend on each key stage. A key question is what do you want your curriculum to say about your school and its culture? Time should be spent considering the powerful knowledge that you want to share with your pupils and, more importantly, to consider why you want them to know this. You should work with subject leads to consider how their curriculum should begin, what pupils need to learn, by when, how, how this interleaves from one lesson, to one week, to one month to the next. You should consider what emphasis you want to place on knowledge comparative to skills. There are huge and powerful decisions to make here. You should also spend time considering very carefully how you want teaching across your school to look. Will there be an institutionalised routine for learning? Or will you leave this to subject areas to choose for themselves?

Workload and training

If you truly value your staff, want to retain your staff and want to support them to ensure that the enacted curriculum is as good as it can be then you really do need to consider workload and training. You need to consider how you use directed time, approaches to marking, how many mock exams and internal assessments you set, your approach to data, co-planning and how many school improvement drivers you are going to enact in any one given academic year. You also need to carefully consider the emphasis you place on training and development for staff. How much time will you give staff to devote to training? How much of your school budget will you devote to training? Who will deliver the training? What do you want the focus to be on?

There are many other factors that allow us to drive a school culture. We do not always have to equate highly professional, slick and 'on it' with high stakes accountability and a climate of measuring everything that moves. Of course, they are points to consider as well. Ultimately, I would argue that all school cultures are a manifestation of the principal/head's will, personality and approach. I am yet to work in a school where this is not the case.

Concluding thoughts

**'We do not learn from experience... we learn from reflecting on that experience.'
– John Dewey**

In my closing thoughts, I return to my starting point, the reason why I decided to write about the CRAFT of assessment. I hope that after reading this book it will provide a platform for teachers and leaders in all phases of education to support and enable pupils to become lifelong learners and feel empowered to use assessment in and out of the classroom as a tool for learning. As educators, we want pupils to become immersed in their learning journey and know how the different threads of their curriculum tapestry are weaved together. This is where the CRAFT can empower teachers and leaders to take control and use assessment to know what has been learnt and how we can support pupils in improving their subsequent work to close the knowledge gap.